FRESH ITALIAN

MARINA FILIPPELLI

hamlyn

Note

Both metric and imperial measurements have been given in all recipes. Use one set of measurements only, and not a mixture of both.

Standard level spoon measurements are used in all recipes.

1 tablespoon = one 15 ml spoon

1 teaspoon = one 5 ml spoon

Ovens should be preheated to the specified temperature – if using a fan-assisted oven, follow the manufacturer's instructions for adjusting the time and the temperature.

Fresh herbs should be used unless otherwise stated.

Medium eggs should be used unless otherwise stated.

The Department of Health advises that eggs should not be consumed raw. This book contains some dishes made with raw or lightly cooked eggs. It is prudent for vulnerable people such as pregnant and nursing mothers, invalids, the elderly, babies and young children to avoid uncooked or lightly cooked dishes made with eggs. Once prepared, these dishes should be kept refrigerated and used promptly.

This book includes dishes made with nuts and nut derivatives. It is advisable for those with known allergic reactions to nuts and nut derivatives and those who may be potentially vulnerable to these allergies, such as pregnant and nursing mothers, invalids, the elderly, babies and children to avoid dishes made with nuts and nut oils. It is also prudent to check the labels of pre-prepared ingredients for the possible inclusion of nut derivatives.

First published in Great Britain in 2006 by
Hamlyn, a division of Octopus Publishing Group Ltd
2–4 Heron Quays, London E14 4JP

Copyright © Octopus Publishing Group Ltd 2006

ISBN-13: 978-0-600-61497-5
ISBN-10: 0-600-61497-2

A CIP catalogue record for this book is available from the British Library

Printed and bound in China

10 9 8 7 6 5 4 3 2 1

Contents

Introduction

We all strive for good health and vitality, and while we are aware that what we eat every day has more impact on our health than anything else, our busy, stressful lives invariably get between us and our best intentions. A succession of trendy diets has not provided the answer. They might help trim our waistlines but they are not always healthy, and because they often involve sacrificing some of our favourite foods, their success is often short-lived. The long-term solution has to be balance. A healthy, balanced diet that doesn't rely on willpower but is based on delicious, wholesome freshly cooked ingredients is worth a thousand trends!

The Italian approach to food and drink offers just that – a balanced diet based on a daily consumption of pasta, rice or polenta, good-quality fish or meat, plus an abundance of ripe seasonal fruit and vegetables. Add to that the ace card of Italian cooking – freshness – and you are halfway there.

Freshness is paramount in all stages of Italian cooking and this begins with the shopping. Italians still have a close relationship with the ingredients they buy, expecting the best from their suppliers. They don't want cellophane-wrapped vegetables that you cannot touch or smell in order to assess their ripeness. Nor are they interested in being able to eat anything they want all year round. In Italy, what you buy depends on what is freshly available and at its seasonal best. Sometimes this will mean that you won't be able to get the artichokes you crave or the mushrooms you were planning to use for a risotto. Frustrating perhaps, but at least you can cook in the knowledge that what you are preparing is in its ripe and tasty prime, and that it won't disappoint.

When such attention is given to the quality of ingredients, it is not surprising that freshly cooked meals are still the norm in Italian families. Although convenience foods are slowly creeping on to supermarket shelves, they are still a curiosity and the three rings of the microwave is certainly not the sound that announces dinner is ready. When an Italian family is called to the table with the cry of '*a tavola*', you can guarantee that they will be sharing a meal that has been prepared from scratch with fresh ingredients – much better for your health than so-called convenience foods, which are often packed with salt, fat and additives.

This approach also translates into the Italian preference for fresh, simple flavours. Freshly prepared and wholesome ingredients don't need elaborate sauces or complicated combinations. The Italian way is to allow the clean, distinct flavours of the ingredients to speak for themselves – a style that is reflected in the recipes that are featured in this book.

Although this is not a diet book, it concentrates on healthy recipes in the Italian repertoire. Both traditional and modern recipes have been adapted to lower their calorie and fat contents wherever possible, without compromising on flavour or authenticity.

Eating as a way of life

Italians love their food and conversations at the table often revolve around what wonderful supplier someone might have discovered, the best way to prepare an ingredient or an amazing meal somebody might have had or plans to have in the near future. In fact, the dining table is the hub of social interaction and family life.

Breakfast generally consists of a cappuccino or espresso with biscuits or a *brioche*, which in Italy is more like a croissant. Lunch and dinner are not dissimilar in their structure. Traditionally, they can be split into four courses: *antipasto*, *primo piatto*, *secondo piatto* and the *dolce*. The *antipasto* (starter) can either be one dish, such as Prawn and Borlotti Salad (*see page 30*), or a combination of lots of little dishes, served tapas style and referred to in the plural as *antipasti*. Then comes the *primo piatto* (first course), which will be pasta, soup, risotto or polenta, depending on personal and regional preferences. The *secondo piatto* (second course) is a meat or fish dish accompanied by a vegetable or salad. Finally, comes the *dolce* (dessert), which is hardly ever skipped, but will more often than not consist of a fresh fruit salad or a bowl of fresh fruit taken to the table for everyone to tuck into. Bread and wine are a constant at the Italian table, and most people complete their meal with a shot of espresso.

Nowadays not all meals consist of so many courses. Often you might just have pasta and a meat dish, then perhaps fruit. Alternatively, you could opt for a bowl of pasta, then a side vegetable. A heavy lunch could be followed by just a wholesome minestrone (*see page 53*) for dinner. Whatever the meal, however, it is unlikely that an Italian will ever leave the table having only eaten a huge bowl of pasta or a big steak – that just wouldn't be balanced enough and they have too healthy a relationship with food for that.

Equipment

You won't need any expensive or unusual equipment to make the recipes in this book. All the tools listed here can be found in any good kitchen store.

SAUCEPANS It really is worth investing in heavy-based saucepans with tight-fitting lids. The heavy base ensures that heat is evenly distributed, while the lid is used in some recipes for trapping any moisture from the food in the pan.

NONSTICK FRYING PAN This is not strictly essential, but can be extremely helpful when trying to cut down on the quantity of oil or butter used in cooking.

RIDGED CAST-IRON GRIDDLE PAN A great way of cooking steaks, chops, chicken breasts, chunky fish steaks and vegetables without the need for oil. The pan must be heated until smoking hot to sear the ingredients quickly and achieve the desired charred flavour and griddle marks.

KITCHEN KNIVES There is no need for a domestic cook to have a huge selection of kitchen knives. All you need is a large cook's

knife for slicing and chopping (this also comes in handy for bruising garlic) and a small paring knife for slicing and chopping smaller ingredients. A small serrated knife for cutting tomatoes and fruit is also useful, as is a large serrated bread knife.

LARGE COLANDER If you are going to cook pasta regularly, then you will need a large colander to drain it swiftly and efficiently. Once you have established that your pasta is perfectly cooked *al dente*, it will need instant draining, and a large colander is the most practical and sensible, as it gives you enough space to give the pasta a good shake and remove any excess water. The colander will also come in handy for draining pulses and washing salads and vegetables.

PIZZA, PASTA AND PASTRY WHEELS Pizza wheels make light work of cutting pizzas into wedges – much easier than struggling with a knife! Smaller wheels are more suitable for precise work like cutting pasta for ravioli or tortellini. Whether you use plain or fluted cutters is a matter of aesthetic preference.

GRATER The most versatile graters are the large ones with four faces – these can be used for all grating jobs, whether nutmeg, lemon rind or Parmesan cheese, giving you the freedom to choose your desired grade. Hand-held Microplane® graters are also very good – extra sharp, they make grating effortless.

TONGS These are great for lifting and turning pieces of food in frying pans, griddle pans or on the barbecue. They can also be used for tossing sauces into, and serving, long pasta shapes such as spaghetti or fettuccine.

PASTA MACHINE These are inexpensive and make light work of the otherwise tough job of rolling out the pasta dough with a rolling pin. The attachments that cut the pasta sheets into fettuccine and tagliatelle are also great time savers.

Techniques

The recipes in this book come with a detailed explanation on how to prepare the ingredients. Below are certain techniques which are used in more than one recipe.

CLEANING LIVE CLAMS Wash the clams under cold running water, discarding any with broken shells or that remain open when tapped. Soak in plenty of cold water for 30 minutes, then drain and rinse again in cold running water. Place in a bowl and cover with a wet tea towel; keep refrigerated until needed.

CLEANING LIVE MUSSELS Scrub the mussels under cold running water. Pull away the beards attached to the shells and discard any mussels with open shells or that are broken or don't close when tapped. Soak and refrigerate as for cleaning clams (see above).

CLEANING SQUID Clean squid under cold running water. Pull the tentacles away from the body. The squid's entrails will come out easily. Discard the clear piece of cartilage inside the body cavity. Wash the body well, discarding the pinkish membrane. Cut between the tentacles and head. Discard the head and entrails.

DEVEINING KING PRAWNS To devein peeled prawns, make a cut along the back of each prawn with a small, sharp knife and pull away and discard the dark intestinal tract. To devein prawns to be cooked in their shells, make a small incision between shell segments and gently pull away and discard the intestinal tract.

SKINNING TOMATOES Place the tomatoes in a heatproof bowl and pour in enough boiling water to cover them. Leave for 30 seconds until the skin has loosened, then drain. When cool enough to handle, cut a small cross at the base of each tomato, then peel off and discard the skin.

BRUISING GARLIC CLOVES Place the peeled garlic clove on a chopping board, then lay the flat side of a large knife on it, covering the garlic. Push down on the flat of the knife blade with the palm of your hand until you feel the garlic give slightly, then use as per the recipe.

The Italian larder

Shopping for Italian ingredients couldn't be easier. It used to be that you had to go exclusively to Italian delis for good quality produce, but these days most supermarkets stock well-sourced ingredients from reputable producers. If you shop for these basic ingredients with care, you'll be halfway to a great Italian gastronomic experience.

PASTA Pasta is eaten throughout Italy, with different regions favouring different shapes and sauces. It can be made with or without egg, using durum wheat and/or soft wheat flour, and cooked from fresh or dried. Italians have strong opinions as to what pasta to use with which sauce and any general rule as to which criteria to use when making your choice will be compromised by so many exceptions that your best guide is tradition. So go with what recipes suggest and what you see being used in restaurants in Italy. Buy the best you can afford and stick to Italian brands.

People often have the misconception that fresh pasta is superior or somehow more sophisticated than dried pasta. This could not be further from the truth. Fresh pasta is reserved for specific shapes and sauces, and is most frequently eaten in central Italy. In certain regions of southern Italy, such as Sicily, people who eat pasta every day might never even have tasted it fresh!

RISOTTO RICE Risotto rice is now readily available in supermarkets and delis, so there is no need to attempt making risotto with any other rice. Avoid generically labelled risotto rice and go instead for one of three specific varieties grown in the Po Valley: vialone nano, arborio or carnaroli. Stirring risotto as it cooks helps the grains release their starch and it is this that makes the final result so creamy. In order to make risottos healthier, the recipes in this book suggest making them without the addition of butter, and when using this method, vialone nano, with its higher starch content, gives a creamier result.

POLENTA Polenta is a coarsely ground corn flour that is cooked in water to make soft polenta to serve with meat, vegetables or seafood. Once cold, soft polenta sets into a firm block that can be topped with other ingredients and grilled, as in Polenta with Parma Ham, Asparagus and Fontina (*see page 60*) or sliced and griddled as in Grilled Polenta with Wild Mushrooms (*see page 59*). Raw polenta takes about 40 minutes to cook, but you can get very good results with the instant polenta most Italians use in everyday cooking. It takes 5 minutes to cook instant polenta and for this reason we have opted to use it in the recipes in this book.

CHEESES

Fontina This is a mild cheese from Piedmont, which melts evenly and smoothly, making it perfect for cooking.

Mozzarella This can be made from cows' milk or water buffalo milk (*mozzarella di bufala*). Cows' milk mozzarella is more than adequate to use in cooking when it is going to be melted, but if you are planning to eat your mozzarella fresh in a tomato and mozzarella salad or using it to make Parma Ham and Buffalo Mozzarella *Involtini* (*see page 32*), it is worth splashing out on buffalo mozzarella; it tastes fresher and creamier. Only buy mozzarella kept in water.

Parmesan *Parmigiano Reggiano* is a cows' milk cheese made in Emilia-Romagna. It is used extensively grated on to pasta, stirred into risottos or shaved on to salads. It is also delicious broken into small pieces and eaten as a nibble with a glass of red wine. *Grana Padano* is similar to Parmesan cheese and a more economical choice for cooking.

Pecorino This is a sheep's milk cheese made in central and southern Italy. There are different varieties, which can be aged until they are ready for the table or matured further until dry and crumbly, to be used grated in cooking.

Ricotta This is a naturally low-fat soft cheese made from the whey left over from cheese making. The whey is reheated, then strained into baskets to drain, hence the name ricotta, which literally means 'recooked'. The most commonly found ricotta outside Italy is made from cows' milk and it is the one recommended for the recipes in this book.

BUTTER Butter is not as widely used as olive oil. In the north of Italy it is sometimes used for softening vegetables, pan-frying and browning meat for stews or braised meats. It is also used to add the finishing touch to risottos and polenta. Except for the odd recipe, southern regions traditionally only really use it in baking. Any recipe in this book that would traditionally call for the use of butter has been adapted, replacing the butter with another ingredient, to lower its saturated fat content.

OLIVE OIL You can't cook Italian food without olive oil! It features in most recipes (sometimes even in cakes and biscuits) and is used in every region of the country. There are different grades of olive oil. Extra virgin olive oil is made from the first cold pressing of olives and its rich flavour can vary from peppery to nutty or grassy. It is generally used to dress salads, or drizzled over dishes at the end of cooking. Whatever style you prefer,

make sure you get estate-bottled extra virgin, and if you are unsure, use price as your guide – it is always worth spending a little more. Use regular, commercially produced olive oil for cooking, as it is lighter in flavour and less expensive.

Is all this oil good for us? Essentially, yes. All plant oils are a good source of vitamin E and essential fatty acids, which help reduce the risk of heart attack. Olive oil contains mostly monounsaturated fats, unlike sunflower or corn oil, which are higher in polyunsaturated fats. From a health perspective, this is significant. When exposed to heat, polyunsaturates generate free radicals, which have been linked to heart disease and cancer, while monounsaturated oils are less vulnerable to free radical generation. Nevertheless, too much fat is not recommended and oil is also highly calorific. All the recipes in this book use minimal amounts when cooking and a light drizzle of flavoursome raw extra virgin olive oil is recommended as a finishing touch to some dishes.

FLOURS Italians generally use two types of soft wheat flour. They are graded as 0 flour, which is similar to regular plain flour, and 00, which is ground finer and the preferred choice for making fresh pasta and cakes. 00 flour can be bought in Italian delis and some good supermarkets. Another flour commonly used is

semola di grano duro, a durum wheat flour used in breads and pasta. It is finer than the semolina generally used in other countries, so it is worth buying it from Italian delis, especially when making silky smooth pasta.

HAM *Prosciutto* is the generic Italian word for ham. *Prosciutto crudo* (literally meaning 'raw ham') is the most commonly known Italian ham, of which the most famous variety is *Prosciutto di Parma* (or Parma ham). It is a raw ham cured in salt, then hung to dry and age. What makes Parma ham so particular is that it is made with the hind legs of pigs fed on the whey left over from making Parmesan cheese, making it sweeter than other *prosciutti crudi*. *Prosciutto cotto* is cooked ham.

ANCHOVIES Most commonly used in southern cooking, anchovies can be bought fresh or preserved in salt or oil. Salted anchovies taste fresher than those preserved in oil, but need thorough rinsing to remove the salt. The flavour and saltiness of preserved anchovies can be mellowed by soaking them in milk. Unless a recipe specifies fresh anchovies, use the preserved fish.

TOMATOES There is an abundant variety of tomatoes available in Italy in summer, from juicy plum tomatoes to sweet cherry tomatoes and green salad tomatoes. Each variety has its own use and it is the San Marzano plum tomatoes that are prized for making sauces. These are the tomatoes most commonly used skinned in cans – be it chopped or whole. Good-quality canned tomatoes should not be frowned upon and Italians happily use them in winter to make their sauces. In fact, you are better off using canned rather than unripened acidic greenhouse tomatoes any day! Passata is smooth, raw puréed tomatoes sold bottled or in cartons to use in cooking.

MUSHROOMS The most widely available wild mushrooms found in Italy are porcini, chanterelles and girolles. During their short season in late summer and autumn, they are eaten raw in salads,

CHILLIES AND BLACK PEPPER Chillies are particularly popular in southern Italy, where they are used fresh or dried to add a little heat to dishes. Black pepper is only sparingly used and mostly in the north. Actually, most Italians tend to laugh at waiters in Italian restaurants abroad, armed with their pepper mills.

VINEGAR Red wine vinegar is the most commonly used vinegar for dressing salads or for cooking. Balsamic vinegar, made in Modena, is also popular, but it is only really worth buying good-quality aged balsamic, which should be rich, sweet and syrupy. The real thing can be very pricey, but a little goes a long way with balsamic, and just a few drops are enough to enliven a salad, sauce or even a bowl of fresh strawberries as in Strawberries with Balsamic Vinegar (*see page 148*).

SALT Salt has been medically proven to be associated with high blood pressure and heart disease, so it is advisable only to season food lightly with it. There are some easy steps that you can take to help lower the amount of salt that you use when cooking Italian food:

ONE Season the food very lightly during initial cooking, then taste the dish at the end, after all the ingredients have been added and cooked through. The flavours of the dish will develop during cooking and any sauce will have reduced, probably making it unnecessary to season any further. If you are too heavy-handed during initial cooking, you could over-season. **TWO** Make your own pasta sauces and stocks, as shop-bought ones often contain excessive salt, as well as additives. **THREE** Slowly cut back on the quantity of salt you use on a daily basis. If you do so gradually, your tastebuds will naturally become accustomed to eating food with less salt. **FOUR** Flavour food with fresh herbs, garlic, chilli, black pepper and lemon rind to add interest and mask the fact that you are using less salt. A light drizzle of extra virgin olive oil, added at the table, also helps.

pan-fried with garlic and stirred into pasta, eaten on bruschetta or polenta, used in risottos or served with sliced steak. At any other time of the year, Italians rely on dried mushrooms that need soaking in hot water before cooking. Of these, porcini are the most popular; stirred into stews, soups and risottos or even delicious pan-fried with the most mundane of field mushrooms. Make sure that you make use of the soaking water from mushrooms, as it is packed with flavour.

OLIVES Black and green olives are commonly marinated in olive oil and herbs to be eaten as part of an *antipasto* selection. Many Italian recipes also call for them, especially in pizzas, breads and pasta dishes.

CAPERS Capers are small flower buds preserved in salt or vinegar. Soak them in cold water to remove the saltiness or sharpness from the vinegar before using. Small capers are generally more flavoursome than larger buds.

PULSES Borlotti beans, cannellini beans, chickpeas and lentils are very popular in soups, stews and salads. The beans and chickpeas are eaten fresh when in season, but when cooking them from dry, they will need soaking overnight in cold water. Pulses are a great source of protein.

Menu plans

When you are planning your menu, include more than one course by choosing recipes from our different chapters. That doesn't mean you need to make things complicated for yourself. For instance, when making a risotto, choose a *secondo piatto* that won't require too much last-minute attention. Here are just a few suggestions, with different occasions in mind. Double up recipes according to the number of people you are serving.

WEEKDAY FAMILY LUNCH FOR 4–6 PEOPLE

Panzanella (*see page 36*)

Pea, Broad Bean and Basil Frittata (*see page 40*)
Braised Artichokes with Mint (*see page 110*)
Rustic Loaf (*see page 130*)

FAMILY DINNER 1 FOR 4 PEOPLE

Spring Minestrone (*see page 53*)

Grilled Pork Steaks with Sage (*see page 106*)
Broccoli with Garlic and Chilli (*see page 113*)

Affogato al Caffè (*see page 150*)

FAMILY DINNER 2 FOR 4 PEOPLE

Spaghetti with Clams (*see page 47*)

Grilled Red Mullet with Thyme and Lemon (*see page 76*)
Fennel, Orange and Olive Salad (*see page 34*)

Sorbetto al Limone with Wild Strawberries (*see page 155*)

SUNDAY LUNCH FOR 6 PEOPLE

Grilled Peppers with Anchovy, Chilli, Garlic and Parsley
(*see page 22*)
Sweet and Sour Baby Onions (*see page 27*)
Rustic Loaf (*see page 130*)

Fettuccine with Ragu (*see page 46*)
Roast Rabbit with Rosemary and White Wine (*see page 104*)
Braised Black Cabbage with Chilli and Fennel Seeds
(*see page 118*)

Pecorino, Pears and Honey (*see page 154*)

LARGE GATHERING FOR 8–10 PEOPLE

Bruschetta (*see page 26*)

Bollito Misto with Salsa Verde (*see page 107*)

Pecorino, Pears and Honey (*see page 154*) and/or a selection
of sorbets and granitas (*see pages 144–147*)

DINNER PARTY FOR 4–6 PEOPLE

Parma Ham and Buffalo Mozzarella *Involtini* (*see page 32*)

Lemony Prawn and Pea Risotto (*see page 62*)
Monkfish Skewers Wrapped in Prosciutto (*see page 78*)
Baked Tomatoes with Breadcrumbs (*see page 117*)

Blood Orange Granita (*see page 144*)

Basic recipes

Every Italian cook has his or her favourite basic staple recipes. Here is our selection that will be referred to regularly throughout the book. Follow them carefully the first few times, then once you're confident preparing them, feel free to experiment. Add a little extra flour to the Basic Pasta Dough on a warm humid day or give the Salsa Verde an extra kick by adding extra capers and garlic.

Basic pizza dough

INGREDIENTS *7 g (¼ oz) fresh yeast or 1 teaspoon dried yeast* ‖ *pinch of caster sugar* ‖ *500 g (1 lb) plain flour, plus extra for dusting* ‖ *350 ml (12 fl oz) lukewarm water* ‖ *1½ teaspoons salt* ‖ *olive oil, for oiling*

ONE Dissolve the yeast in a bowl with the sugar, 2 tablespoons of the flour and 50 ml (2 fl oz) of the measurement water. Leave to stand for 5 minutes until it starts to form bubbles, then add the remaining water. Add the salt and half the remaining flour and stir with one hand until you have a paste-like mixture. Gradually add all the remaining flour, working the mixture until you have a moist dough. Shape the dough into a ball, cover with a moist cloth and leave to rest in a warm place for 5 minutes. **TWO** Lightly dust a work surface with flour and knead the dough for 10 minutes until smooth and elastic. Shape into 4 equal-sized balls and place spaced apart on a lightly oiled baking sheet. Cover with a moist cloth and leave to rise in a warm place for 1 hour. Use according to your recipe.

Basic pasta dough

This basic recipe, using two eggs, makes about 300 g (10 oz) pasta dough, which is sufficient when making stuffed pasta for six people. When making tagliatelle or fettuccine for four people, you will need 400 g (13 oz) pasta dough, using three eggs as described below.

INGREDIENTS *150 g (5 oz) Italian 00 flour or fine plain flour* ‖ *50 g (2 oz)* semola di grano duro, *plus extra for dusting* ‖ *2 eggs*

ONE Combine the flour and *semola* in a large bowl. Make a well in the centre and break in the eggs. Mix the eggs in with your fingers, gradually drawing in the flour. Once the central mixture becomes too thick to handle, use the heel of your hand to knead and bring the mixture together. Alternatively, place all the ingredients in a food processor and pulse until combined. **TWO** Tip the dough on to a clean work surface and knead for 3–4 minutes until smooth and elastic. Wrap in clingfilm and chill for at least 30 minutes, or up to 4 hours. **THREE** Set your pasta machine up at the largest opening. Cut the pasta dough into quarters and pick up one piece, keeping the remaining dough covered with clingfilm. Shape the dough you are holding into a rough rectangle and run it through the machine. Fold it in half widthways and run it through again. Lower the setting on the machine by one notch and run the dough through again. Continue running the dough once through each of the remaining settings. If the pasta sheet becomes too long to handle, cut it in half and run one half through at a time. **FOUR** Lay the pasta sheet on a work surface dusted with *semola*, then cover with a tea towel while you roll out the remaining dough. Use according to your recipe.

MAKING LARGER QUANTITIES The basic ratio for pasta dough is one egg for 100 g (3½ oz) flour, so if making a three-egg pasta dough, use the following quantities:

225 g (7½ oz) Italian 00 flour or fine plain flour ‖ *75 g (3 oz)* semola di grano duro ‖ *3 eggs*

EXTRA LIGHT EGG-FREE PASTA DOUGH Fresh pasta can also be made using water in the place of eggs. All you have to do is replace each egg with 60 ml (2½ fl oz) water at room temperature. The result is a lot more delicate and obviously lower in fat, but it can be harder to handle, so it is best that you become proficient in making the basic pasta dough before attempting this dough.

Basic tomato sauce

INGREDIENTS *2 teaspoons olive oil* ‖ *1 garlic clove, finely chopped* ‖ *1 kg (2 lb) canned chopped tomatoes* ‖ *large pinch of caster sugar* ‖ *5 basil leaves (optional)* ‖ *salt*

ONE Heat the oil in a heavy-based saucepan over a medium heat and stir in the garlic. Cook for 30 seconds, stirring, then add the tomatoes, sugar and basil, if using. Season lightly with salt and bring to the boil. **TWO** You now have two options. If you want a very light sauce to spoon over stuffed fresh pasta or if your sauce will be used in another recipe where it will undergo further cooking, simmer the sauce over a medium heat for 2–3 minutes. Alternatively, if you are aiming for a more robust, concentrated tomato sauce to stir into pasta, simmer the sauce over a low heat for 40–45 minutes until thick and rich. The sauce can be eaten chunky or blended in a food processor or blender until smooth, then reheated.

Salsa verde

This gutsy fresh herb sauce is delicious served with meats and grilled fish, and is a classic accompaniment to *Bollito Misto* (*see page 107*). This sharp, vinegary version is particularly good at cutting through the richness of red meat.

INGREDIENTS *2 garlic cloves, finely chopped* ‖ *3 anchovy fillets in olive oil, drained and finely chopped* ‖ *1 tablespoon capers, soaked, drained and finely chopped* ‖ *4 tablespoons roughly chopped flat leaf parsley* ‖ *3 tablespoons roughly chopped mint* ‖ *1 tablespoon red wine vinegar* ‖ *4 tablespoons extra virgin olive oil, plus extra if storing* ‖ *salt and pepper (optional)*

ONE Combine all the ingredients in a small bowl and adjust the seasoning to taste. If you are not serving the Salsa Verde straight away, spoon it into a sterilized glass jar and pour in a layer of oil. This will protect the sauce from coming into contact with air. Cover and store in the refrigerator for up to 2 weeks.

Homemade stocks

It is not strictly necessary to make your own stock, now that supermarkets and delis offer such a huge variety, but if you do have the time, making your own stock can be very satisfying. It gives you the confidence that only the best ingredients have gone into it and that no unnecessary fat, salt or additives have been used. It is also reassuring to remember that, although the stock pot needs to bubble away for a long time, it requires very little supervision.

Basic vegetable stock

This basic recipe can be adapted to make all the other stocks used in this book (see right). It is made with absolutely no salt, so you can decide how to season, according to the recipe in which it will be used.

INGREDIENTS *1 large onion, roughly chopped* ‖ *2 carrots, roughly chopped* ‖ *2 celery sticks, roughly chopped* ‖ *2 leeks, roughly chopped* ‖ *1 fennel bulb, roughly chopped* ‖ *2 bay leaves* ‖ *handful of parsley stalks* ‖ *2 sprigs of thyme* ‖ *6 black peppercorns* ‖ *1 tablespoon groundnut oil* ‖ *4 litres (7 pints) water at room temperature*

ONE Place the vegetables, herbs and peppercorns in a large saucepan. Stir in the oil, cover and cook over a medium heat, stirring occasionally, for about 10 minutes, until the vegetables are softened and just beginning to colour. **TWO** Pour in the measurement water and bring to the boil over a high heat. Skim off any scum that rises to the surface, then simmer, uncovered, over a medium heat for 1 hour, skimming occasionally. Set aside to cool. **THREE** Strain the stock into a clean pan. Boil vigorously until reduced by half. Once cooled, store the stock in a covered container in the refrigerator or transfer to small freezerproof containers and freeze.

Stock variations

Some recipes call for the use of chicken, beef or fish stock. Once you've mastered making vegetable stock you'll find it easy to adapt the basic recipe to make these different flavoured stocks. You'll need all the ingredients listed in the Basic Vegetable Stock recipe, with the addition of the ingredients mentioned below.

Chicken stock

ONE Cut **2 uncooked chicken carcasses** into large pieces and place in a large saucepan with the measurement water. Bring to the boil over a high heat, skim, then stir in the remaining ingredients, omitting the oil. Simmer, uncovered, for 2 hours, skimming occasionally, then strain and reduce as opposite.

Beef stock

ONE Trim away any fat from **2 kg (4 lb) beef bones**. Place in a large roasting tin and roast in a preheated oven, 220°C (425°F), Gas Mark 7, for 45 minutes–1 hour until golden brown, turning occasionally. **TWO** Transfer the bones to a large saucepan and add the water. Bring to the boil over a high heat, skim, then stir in the remaining ingredients, omitting the oil. Simmer, uncovered, for 4 hours, skimming occasionally, then strain and reduce as opposite.

Fish stock

ONE Wash **2 kg (4 lb) bones and heads of non-oily fish** and place in a large saucepan with **750 ml (1¼ pints) dry white wine**. Stir in the remaining ingredients, omitting the oil, and just enough water to cover. Bring to the boil, skim, then simmer, uncovered, for 30 minutes. Strain and reduce as opposite.

Antipasti – starters,
salads and frittatas

Grilled peppers with anchovy, chilli, garlic and parsley

This southern Italian dish is gorgeous served with grilled crusty bread to soak up all the juices. For a plainer version leave out the anchovies, or make this *antipasto* even punchier by adding a handful of capers.

INGREDIENTS *4 large red peppers* ‖ *3 anchovy fillets, in salt or olive oil* ‖ *1 garlic clove, finely sliced* ‖ *pinch of crushed dried red chillies* ‖ *2 tablespoons roughly chopped flat leaf parsley* ‖ *2 tablespoons extra virgin olive oil* ‖ *salt*

ONE Place the whole peppers on a baking sheet and cook under a preheated very hot grill, on the highest shelf possible, until the skin is completely black and blistered, then turn the peppers and cook until evenly charred all over. **TWO** Remove the peppers and leave only until cool enough to handle, then peel off the skin. If this proves difficult, enclose the peppers in a freezer bag and leave to steam for 5 minutes so that the skin loosens further. Cut the peppers in half, remove and discard the stalk, core and seeds and cut the flesh into 2.5 cm (1 inch) strips. Place in a non-reactive dish. **THREE** If using salted anchovies, rinse well under cold running water; anchovies in oil will only need draining. Halve the fillets, then add to the peppers with the remaining ingredients. Season with salt and toss gently, then cover and leave to marinate in the refrigerator for at least 4 hours. The peppers will keep, covered, in the refrigerator for up to 1 week, but let them come to room temperature before serving.

Serves 4 as part of an antipasto *selection*

NUTRIENT ANALYSIS PER SERVING 376 kJ – 90 kcal – 2 g protein – 7 g carbohydrate – 6 g sugars – 6 g fat – 1 g saturates – 2 g fibre – 94 mg sodium

HEALTHY TIP Peppers contain very high levels of vitamin C, together with betacarotene (especially high in red peppers), which is converted by the body into vitamins A and E – in fact, all the antioxidant vitamins are present in this single highly concentrated source. Peppers also contain zinc.

Marinated anchovies

The only 'cooking' these anchovies get is from the lemon-based marinade, so only make this dish if you can lay your hands on the freshest fish. Small sardines or small raw shelled prawns are also delicious prepared in this way.

INGREDIENTS *1 kg (2 lb) fresh anchovies ‖ 1 red chilli, finely chopped ‖ 2 garlic cloves, finely chopped ‖ 1 tablespoon roughly chopped flat leaf parsley ‖ 4 tablespoons extra virgin olive oil ‖ 2 lemons, halved ‖ salt ‖ crusty bread, to serve*

ONE To fillet the anchovies, lift back their heads, pulling their heads and spine up and away from their bodies, then cut off their tails. You will now have flat, triangular-shaped anchovies. Rinse under cold running water, then pat dry with kitchen paper. **TWO** Place one-third of the anchovies in a non-reactive dish in which they fit snugly in a single layer. Season with salt, then scatter with one-third of the chilli, garlic and parsley. Pour over 1 tablespoon of the oil and squeeze over the juice from one of the lemon halves. Repeat the layers until all the ingredients have been used up, with the final layer having 2 tablespoons of oil and the juice of a whole lemon. **THREE** Cover and leave to marinate in the refrigerator for at least 2 hours or up to 8 hours or overnight. Serve with bread as part of an *antipasto* selection.

Serves 4–6 as part of an antipasto *selection*

NUTRIENT ANALYSIS PER SERVING 1467 kJ – 350 kcal – 31 g protein – 1 g carbohydrate – 1 g sugars – 5 g fat – 6 g saturates – 0 g fibre – 180 mg sodium

HEALTHY TIP Anchovies (and sardines) are fatty fish and contain omega-3 fatty acids, which protect against heart disease and some forms of cancer. Although this delicious dish has a high fat content due to the fish and olive oil (which is high in monounsaturates), it could help to control blood cholesterol.

Bruschetta

In the height of summer, when tomatoes are at their sweetest and juiciest, this poor man's dish becomes the most divine crowd pleaser. It might seem like an obvious recipe, but precise execution is essential. Give the tomatoes time to release their juices, and if they are not perfectly ripe, cheat, adding sweetness with a little pinch of sugar. The flavour benefits from slightly charred bread that is dry enough so that it will hold its shape as it soaks in the tomato juices, but not so much that you can't bite into it. It is an art that benefits from lots of practice!

INGREDIENTS *400 g (13 oz) very ripe tomatoes, finely chopped* ‖ *2 tablespoons extra virgin olive oil* ‖ *4 slices of crusty bread* ‖ *1 large garlic clove, unpeeled* ‖ *salt*

ONE Place the tomatoes in a bowl, season with salt and stir in the oil. Set aside for at least 15 minutes for the salt to draw out the tomato juices. **TWO** Grill the bread on both sides under a preheated very hot grill, about 7 cm (3 inches) from the heat, until crisp and lightly charred around the edges. Alternatively, griddle or barbecue the bread. **THREE** Rub one side of each slice with the garlic clove (the skin will break as you start rubbing it against the bread), then lay the bread, garlic side up, on a platter. Top with the chopped tomatoes, ensuring that you include the tasty juices, and serve.

Serves 4 as an antipasto *on its own or as part of an* antipasto *selection*

NUTRIENT ANALYSIS PER SERVING 668 kJ – 160 kcal – 4 g protein – 22 g carbohydrate – 4 g sugars – 7 g fat – 1 g saturates – 3 g fibre – 208 mg sodium

HEALTHY TIP Tomatoes are an excellent source of the antioxidants vitamin C and betacarotene. Combine them with garlic – which may help to prevent blood-clotting problems – in this tasty, low-fat starter.

Sweet and sour baby onions

You will need syrupy aged balsamic vinegar for this recipe, and should keep the heat under the pan really low so that the natural sugars in the onions have the chance to caramelize. The slow cooking and good-quality balsamic guarantee a gorgeous glaze without having to use too much sugar. Serve with some crusty bread to mop up the sticky juices. You could also serve the onions with the *Bollito Misto* with Salsa Verde (*see page 107*) – not traditional, but nevertheless delicious!

INGREDIENTS *625 g (1¼ lb) baby onions* ‖ *1 tablespoon olive oil* ‖ *2 tablespoons balsamic vinegar* ‖ *½ teaspoon caster sugar* ‖ *salt and pepper*

ONE To make the onions easier to peel, plunge into boiling water for 30 seconds, then drain. When cool enough to handle, peel off the skins, but avoid trimming the root ends, or the onions will lose their shape during cooking. **TWO** Heat the oil in a large, heavy-based frying pan over a medium heat. Stir in the onions, arranging them in a single layer, then add enough water so that the onions are half immersed in liquid. Bring to a gentle simmer and cook for 30 minutes, stirring occasionally. If most of the liquid evaporates, add a couple of tablespoons of hot water. **THREE** Stir in the balsamic vinegar, sugar and salt and pepper and stir well to combine. Continue to cook, stirring occasionally, for a further 1½ hours, adding more water when the pan dries out, until the onions are soft all the way through and caramelized into a golden colour with a rich glaze. Serve at room temperature as part of an *antipasto* selection.

Serves 4–6 as part of an antipasto *selection*

NUTRIENT ANALYSIS PER SERVING 367 kJ – 88 kcal – 2 g protein – 14 g carbohydrate – 11 g sugars – 3 g fat – 0 g saturates – 2 g fibre – 6 mg sodium

HEALTHY TIP There is evidence that onions may reduce the risk of certain cancers. They may also help to prevent blood clot formation and therefore heart disease. Two compounds in onions, allicin and sulphoraphane, are believed to be the important factors for these health benefits.

Bresaola with fresh ricotta and rocket

Bresaola is a cured meat made from air-dried beef. The most traditional way of serving it is as an *antipasto* with a drizzle of olive oil, some lemon juice and black pepper. Here, the delicate sweetness of the ricotta contrasts with the saltiness of the bresaola, while the rocket adds a fresh pepperiness, making a starter or a light lunch in itself.

INGREDIENTS *20 slices of bresaola, about 150 g (5 oz) total weight* ‖ *50 g (2 oz) wild rocket* ‖ *200 g (7 oz) firm ricotta cheese* ‖ *extra virgin olive oil, for drizzling* ‖ *salt (optional) and pepper* ‖ *lemon wedges, to serve*

ONE Divide the bresaola slices equally between 4 plates. Scatter with the rocket, then place a slice of ricotta on each plate. **TWO** Drizzle lightly with oil, then season with salt, if necessary (bresaola can sometimes already be quite salty), and pepper. **THREE** Serve immediately with some lemon wedges on the side.

Serves 4 as a starter or as a light lunch

NUTRIENT ANALYSIS PER SERVING 760 kJ – 180 kcal – 26 g protein – 1 g carbohydrate – 1 g sugars – 8 g fat – 4 g saturates – 1 g fibre – 68 mg sodium

HEALTHY TIP Lean beef is low in fat and an important source of iron in the diet. Iron from 'haem' (animal) sources is more easily absorbed and used by the body than iron from 'non-haem' (vegetable) sources.

Prawn and borlotti salad

Beans are a staple in the Tuscan diet and they are often eaten in salads with prawns or tuna. It is important to dress this salad when the beans are still warm so that all the flavours are fully absorbed by the beans. This should be a quick recipe to prepare, so opt for fresh or canned beans, rather than dried.

INGREDIENTS *200 g (7 oz) fresh shelled borlotti beans or 300 g (10 oz) canned, drained borlotti beans ‖ 2 tablespoons extra virgin olive oil ‖ 2 garlic cloves, crushed ‖ 1 red chilli, deseeded and finely chopped ‖ 2 celery sticks, thinly sliced ‖ 200 g (7 oz) cooked peeled prawns, tails left on ‖ rind and juice of 1 lemon ‖ 50 g (2 oz) wild rocket ‖ salt*

ONE If using fresh beans, place in a saucepan, add enough cold water to cover by about 5 cm (2 inches) and bring to the boil. Skim off any scum that rises to the surface, then reduce the heat to a simmer and cook, uncovered, for 30 minutes or until tender, then drain. If using canned beans, simply rinse under cold running water before using, then heat gently in a saucepan over a medium heat for 3 minutes. **TWO** Place the oil, garlic and chilli in a large bowl. Stir in the warm beans and celery and season with salt. Leave the salad to cool to room temperature. You can then cover and store in the refrigerator for up to 1 day. **THREE** If you prepared the beans in advance, leave them to return to room temperature before serving. Stir in the prawns and the lemon rind and juice, gently toss in the rocket and serve immediately.

Serves 4 as a light lunch or 4–6 as part of an antipasto *selection*

NUTRIENT ANALYSIS PER SERVING 512 kJ – 122 kcal – 13 g protein – 3 g carbohydrate – 1 g sugars – 7 g fat – 1 g saturates – 3 g fibre – 820 mg sodium

HEALTHY TIP Beans such as borlotti are a good source of fibre and are also an important source of 'non-haem' (vegetable) iron. This form of iron is less easily absorbed by the body than 'haem' (animal) iron, but the presence of vitamin C from the lemon juice in this dish assists the process.

Parma ham and buffalo mozzarella *involtini*

Parma ham and mozzarella are a marriage made in heaven! These little bundles are great as part of a mixed *antipasto* spread. They are also delicious made with Parmesan chunks instead of mozzarella.

INGREDIENTS *6 slices of Parma ham* ‖ *12 baby buffalo mozzarelle, about 125 g (4 oz) total weight* ‖ *salt and pepper* ‖ *extra virgin olive oil, for drizzling (optional)*

ONE Cut the ham slices in half lengthways and wrap each piece around a mozzarella. Season lightly with salt and pepper, then place on a serving platter. **TWO** If you like, lightly drizzle the *involtini* with oil, then serve with some cocktail sticks to help pick them up.

Serves 4–6 as part of an antipasto *selection*

NUTRIENT ANALYSIS PER SERVING 406 kJ – 97 kcal – 10 g protein – 0 g carbohydrate – 0 g sugars – 7 g fat – 3 g saturates – 0 g fibre – 460 mg sodium

HEALTHY TIP Mozzarella cheese made from buffalo milk is lower in fat than some other cheeses, and is an excellent source of calcium, zinc, phosphorus and vitamin A, which is important for the skin and is an antioxidant.

Fennel, orange and olive salad

There is no more refreshing salad on a scorching summer's day than this Sicilian combination. Serve it as part of an *antipasto* table or try it as an accompaniment to Swordfish with Lemon, Olives and Capers (*see page 81*) or Grilled Red Mullet with Thyme and Lemon (*see page 76*).

INGREDIENTS *1 large fennel bulb, about 325 g (11 oz), thinly sliced* ‖ *8–10 black olives* ‖ *1 tablespoon extra virgin olive oil* ‖ *2 tablespoons lemon juice* ‖ *2 oranges* ‖ *salt and pepper*

ONE Toss the fennel with the olives, oil and lemon juice in a large bowl. Season with salt and pepper. **TWO** Working over a bowl to catch the juice and using a serrated knife, cut away the skin and pith of the oranges and slice thinly into rounds. Add the orange slices, along with any juice, to the fennel salad and toss very gently to combine.

Serves 4–6 as an antipasto *selection or as a side dish to fish, poultry or red meats*

NUTRIENT ANALYSIS PER SERVING 350 kJ – 84 kcal – 2 g protein – 8 g carbohydrate – 8 g sugars – 5 g fat – 1 g saturates – 2 g fibre – 435 mg sodium

HEALTHY TIP The combination of fennel and oranges makes this salad a good source of folic acid. Dietary folic acid is very important for cell formation in the body. It is also particularly important for mothers in early pregnancy.

Panzanella

Like many great Italian dishes, this one was born out of hardship. Truly authentic panzanella should be mostly made of stale bread, moistened with just enough tomato and olive oil to disguise the fact that the bread is past its best. Nowadays, though, you will find numerous interpretations, with trendy Roman restaurants even adding king prawns to the salad. Although not as basic as the traditional dish, this variation remains true to the origins of panzanella by using cheap southern Italian ingredients.

INGREDIENTS *3 tablespoons extra virgin olive oil* ‖ *1 tablespoon red wine vinegar* ‖ *2 garlic cloves, crushed* ‖ *½ red onion, thinly sliced* ‖ *500 g (1 lb) tomatoes, cut into wedges* ‖ *90 g (3¼ oz) stale crusty bread, crust removed* ‖ *8 large basil leaves, torn* ‖ *40 g (1½ oz) pitted black olives, halved* ‖ *salt*

ONE Place the oil, vinegar, garlic and onion in a large non-reactive salad bowl. Add the tomatoes, season with salt and stir well to combine. **TWO** Cut the bread into 2.5 cm (1 inch) pieces and stir into the salad with the basil and olives. Cover and leave at room temperature for the flavours to develop, stirring occasionally, for 30 minutes–2 hours.

Serves 4–6 as part of an antipasto *selection*

NUTRIENT ANALYSIS PER SERVING 690 kJ – 165 kcal – 3 g protein – 16 g carbohydrate – 5 g sugars – 10 g fat – 2 g saturates – 3 g fibre – 357 mg sodium

HEALTHY TIP Tomatoes contain vitamin C and betacarotene, both of which are valuable antioxidants. They also contain lycopene, which may help to protect against some cancers.

Fresh porcini salad

As salads go, it doesn't get much more extravagant than this! These wild mushrooms can be prohibitively expensive, but one taste of their unique nuttiness and you will know it is worth it. Serve it as a starter or as a side dish to the T-bone *alla Fiorentina* (*see page 101*).

INGREDIENTS *375 g (12 oz) fresh porcini* ‖ *1 lemon, halved* ‖ *1 tablespoon roughly chopped flat leaf parsley* ‖ *2 tablespoons extra virgin olive oil* ‖ *50 g (2 oz) fresh Parmesan cheese shavings* ‖ *salt and pepper*

ONE Brush the mushrooms with a pastry brush to remove any grit, then slice them very thinly. Divide the slices between 4 serving plates. **TWO** Squeeze the juice from the lemon halves over the mushrooms, scatter with the parsley and season with salt and pepper. Drizzle the salad with the oil, then top with the Parmesan shavings. The salad will taste even better after being left to stand for 10 minutes.

Serves 4 as an antipasto *on its own or as a side dish to poultry or red meats*

NUTRIENT ANALYSIS PER SERVING 497 kJ – 120 kcal – 7 g protein – 1 g carbohydrate – 0 g sugars – 10 g fat – 3 g saturates – 2 g fibre – 140 mg sodium

HEALTHY TIP Mushrooms are low in fat and carbohydrate and provide some protein, fibre, vitamins and minerals, including calcium and selenium. However, their light weight means you need to eat a large volume of these fungi to get much nutritional benefit.

Courgette and mint frittata

The sweet, vibrant flavour of mint is the ideal partner for spring and summer vegetables. Like basil, its freshness complements them perfectly. Feel free to substitute the mint with basil, or vice versa in the other frittata overleaf. If having as a light lunch, serve with a green salad.

INGREDIENTS *2 teaspoons olive oil* ‖ *1 onion, thinly sliced* ‖ *2 courgettes, thinly sliced* ‖ *6 eggs* ‖ *2 tablespoons roughly chopped mint* ‖ *salt and pepper*

ONE Heat the oil in a heavy-based, nonstick 23 cm (9 inch) frying pan with a heatproof handle. Stir in the onion and cook over a low heat, stirring occasionally, for 10 minutes until softened, then stir in the courgettes and cook, stirring, for a further 2 minutes. **TWO** Beat the eggs and mint together in a large bowl and season lightly with salt and pepper. Stir in the cooked vegetables, then pour the mixture into the frying pan and quickly arrange the vegetables so that they are evenly dispersed. Cook over a low heat for 8–10 minutes or until all but the top of the frittata is set. **THREE** Finish cooking under a preheated very hot grill, about 10 cm (4 inches) from the heat, until set but not coloured. Give the pan a shake to loosen the frittata or use a spatula, then transfer to a plate to cool. Serve slightly warm or at room temperature.

Serves 4 as a light lunch or 6–8 as an antipasto *with 2–3 other* antipasti

NUTRIENT ANALYSIS PER SERVING 666 kJ – 160 kcal – 12 g protein – 5 g carbohydrate – 1 g sugars – 11 g fat – 3 g saturates – 0 g fibre – 117 mg sodium

HEALTHY TIP Eggs are a relatively cheap source of good protein and are high in iron and vitamins A and D. Egg yolks do have a high cholesterol content, so you should try to limit the number you eat per week.

Pea, broad bean and basil frittata

Frittate can be made with a variety of ingredients and generally it is the season that dictates what should go into your frittata. This combination is undoubtedly a springtime offering, but with frozen peas and beans substituting their fresh counterparts so successfully, there is no reason why you couldn't enjoy it any time of the year.

INGREDIENTS *125 g (4 oz) shelled fresh or frozen peas* ‖ *125 g (4 oz) shelled fresh or frozen broad beans* ‖ *2 teaspoons olive oil* ‖ *1 large onion, thinly sliced* ‖ *1 small garlic clove, crushed* ‖ *6 eggs* ‖ *2 tablespoons freshly grated Parmesan cheese* ‖ *6 large basil leaves, torn into small pieces* ‖ *salt and pepper*

ONE Cook the peas and beans in 2 separate saucepans of boiling water until just tender. Drain and refresh under cold running water, then drain again. Peel off and discard the skins of the beans. **TWO** Heat the oil in a heavy-based, nonstick 23 cm (9 inch) frying pan with a heatproof handle. Stir in the onion and cook over a low heat, stirring occasionally, for 10 minutes until softened. Add the garlic and cook, stirring, for 1 minute. **THREE** Beat the eggs, Parmesan and basil together in a large bowl and season lightly with salt and pepper. Stir in the cooked peas and beans and onion and garlic, then pour the mixture into the frying pan and quickly arrange the vegetables so that they are evenly dispersed. Cook over a low heat for 8–10 minutes or until all but the top of the frittata is set. **FOUR** Finish cooking under a preheated very hot grill, about 10 cm (4 inches) from the heat, until set but not coloured. Give the pan a shake to loosen the frittata or use a spatula, then transfer to a plate to cool. Serve slightly warm or at room temperature.

Serves 4 as a light lunch or 6–8 as an antipasto *with 2–3 other* antipasti

NUTRIENT ANALYSIS PER SERVING 935 kJ – 225 kcal – 17 g protein – 11 g carbohydrate – 5 g sugars – 13 g fat – 4 g saturates – 2 g fibre – 173 mg sodium

HEALTHY TIP Adding peas and beans to eggs supplements the protein content of both the legumes and the eggs, making a good combination. This dish is also a good source of iron and fibre.

Primi piatti – pasta, soups, risottos and polenta

Pesto *alla Genovese*

In Genoa, the home of pesto, this aromatic pasta is traditionally cooked with potatoes and green beans. This might sound unusual, but it is truly a heavenly combination. Italians like to cook the beans all the way through, but here they are added at the end of cooking to keep their bite and freshness.

INGREDIENTS *75 g (3 oz) basil leaves* ‖ *25 g (1 oz) pine nuts* ‖ *2 garlic cloves, crushed* ‖ *2 tablespoons freshly grated Parmesan, plus extra to serve* ‖ *1 tablespoon freshly grated pecorino cheese* ‖ *3 tablespoons olive oil* ‖ *250 g (8 oz) potatoes, peeled and thinly sliced* ‖ *400 g (13 oz) dried trenette or linguine* ‖ *150 g (5 oz) green beans*

ONE Grind the basil, pine nuts and garlic in a mortar with a pestle until the mixture forms a paste. Stir in the cheeses, then slowly add the oil, a little at a time, stirring continuously with a wooden spoon. Alternatively, blend the basil, pine nuts and garlic in a food processor until the mixture forms a paste. Add the cheeses and process briefly, then, with the motor still running, pour in the oil through the feed tube in a thin, steady stream. **TWO** Cook the potatoes in a large saucepan of salted boiling water for 5 minutes, then add the pasta and cook according to the packet instructions until *al dente.* Add the beans 5 minutes before the end of the cooking time. **THREE** Drain the pasta and vegetables, reserving 2 tablespoons of the cooking water. Return the cooked pasta and vegetables to the pan and stir in the pesto sauce, adding the reserved water to loosen the mixture. Serve immediately, scattered with some extra grated Parmesan.

Serves 4

NUTRIENT ANALYSIS PER SERVING 2414 kJ – 570 kcal – 19 g protein – 88 g carbohydrate – 5 g sugars – 19 g fat – 4 g saturates – 7 g fibre – 200 mg sodium

HEALTHY TIP Garlic helps the immune system to build up high levels of resistance to infection. It is antiviral, antibacterial and antiseptic, as well as antibiotic. It is a great detoxifier and contains a high dose of vitamin C as well as the antioxidant mineral selenium. Garlic is one of the most potent aids to good health that you can find.

Fettuccine with ragu

Ragu (or Bolognese) with homemade egg pasta is a dish for special occasions in Italy, be it a family Sunday lunch or the first course on Christmas Day. The sauce uses less tomato than versions you find abroad and the gentle cooking with milk results in a sweet, delicate flavour.

INGREDIENTS *½ tablespoon olive oil* ‖ *1 onion, finely chopped* ‖ *1 celery stick, finely chopped* ‖ *1 carrot, finely chopped* ‖ *350 g (11½ oz) lean minced beef* ‖ *125 ml (4 fl oz) dry white wine* ‖ *1 bay leaf* ‖ *large pinch of freshly grated nutmeg* ‖ *150 ml (¼ pint) semi-skimmed milk* ‖ *400 g (13 oz) can chopped tomatoes* ‖ *250 ml (8 fl oz) shop-bought or homemade Beef Stock (see page 19)* ‖ *1 quantity 3-egg Basic Pasta Dough (see page 16) or 400 g (13 oz) shop-bought fresh fettuccine* ‖ *semola di grano duro, for dusting (optional)* ‖ *salt* ‖ *freshly grated Parmesan cheese, to serve*

ONE Heat the oil in a large, heavy-based saucepan over a low heat. Add the onion, celery and carrot and cook, stirring occasionally, for 10 minutes until softened but not coloured. Add the meat, season lightly with salt and cook, breaking it up with a wooden spoon, until it loses all its pinkness. **TWO** Pour in the wine and increase the heat to bring the sauce to the boil. Add the bay leaf and nutmeg and simmer until the wine has evaporated. Add the milk and simmer gently until that has evaporated. Add the tomatoes and stock and cook uncovered over a very low heat for at least 3 hours, stirring occasionally. The sauce should be very thick, but if it begins to stick to the base of the pan, add a little water. **THREE** If making your own pasta, roll out following the method on page 16, then run the pasta sheets through the fettuccine setting of your pasta machine. Lay the pasta strands on a baking sheet dusted with *semola* and cover with a clean cloth. **FOUR** Cook the pasta in a large saucepan of salted boiling water for 2–3 minutes until *al dente*, or according to the packet instructions if using shop-bought pasta. Drain, reserving a ladleful of the cooking water, and return the pasta to the pan. Add the ragu and cook, stirring, for 30 seconds. Add the reserved water and stir until the pasta is well coated in the sauce. Serve immediately with Parmesan.

Serves 4

NUTRIENT ANALYSIS PER SERVING 2175 kJ – 515 kcal – 33 g protein – 68 g carbohydrate – 10 g sugars – 12 g fat – 4 g saturates – 5 g fibre – 187 mg sodium

HEALTHY TIP Pasta sauces can be rather high in fat, so this tasty low-fat ragu is worth trying if you need to watch your fat intake. Look for really low-fat minced beef, and do not be too generous with the extra Parmesan cheese.

Spaghetti with clams

This delicious dish is simplicity itself; the only skill lies in ensuring that the clams and pasta are cooked at the same time so that neither are left to overcook. Don't be tempted to serve any Parmesan cheese with *spaghetti alle vongole* – as with any other seafood pasta dish, this would be considered a sacrilege in Italy!

INGREDIENTS *2 tablespoons olive oil* ‖ *2 garlic cloves, thinly sliced* ‖ *½ dried chilli, chopped* ‖ *350 g (11½ oz) dried spaghetti* ‖ *1 kg (2 lb) live clams, cleaned* (see page 9 *)* ‖ *2 tablespoons roughly chopped flat leaf parsley* ‖ *extra virgin olive oil, for drizzling (optional)* ‖ *salt*

ONE Heat the olive oil in the largest frying pan you have (or use a wok) over a low heat. Add the garlic and chilli and leave to infuse for 10 minutes. If the garlic begins to colour, simply remove the pan from the hob and let the flavours infuse in the heat of the pan. **TWO** Cook the pasta in a large saucepan of salted boiling water according to the packet instructions until *al dente*. Drain, reserving a ladleful of the cooking water. **THREE** Meanwhile, increase the heat under the frying pan and add the clams, stirring until they open. This shouldn't take longer than 4–5 minutes. Stir in the drained pasta, reserved water and parsley and toss the pasta over the heat for 30 seconds, to combine all the flavours. Serve immediately with a drizzle of extra virgin olive oil, if you like.

Serves 4

NUTRIENT ANALYSIS PER SERVING 1587 kJ – 375 kcal – 15 g protein – 66 g carbohydrate – 3 g sugars – 8 g fat – 1 g saturates – 5 g fibre – 180 mg sodium

HEALTHY TIP Clams are low in saturated fat and contain the valuable omega-3 fatty acids which help to protect against coronary heart disease. They are also a good source of iron, zinc, selenium and other minerals important for health.

Spaghetti with sea bass and tomato sauce

The better quality the ingredients you use, the less you need to do with them, and this pasta dish is a case in point. Use beautifully sweet, ripe tomatoes and the freshest sea bass for this simple yet impressive first course.

INGREDIENTS *2 whole garlic cloves* ‖ *1 tablespoon olive oil* ‖ *¼ teaspoon crushed dried red chillies* ‖ *700 g (1 lb 6 oz) ripe tomatoes, skinned (*see page 9*) and roughly chopped* ‖ *125 ml (4 fl oz) dry white wine* ‖ *350 g (11½ oz) dried spaghetti* ‖ *300 g (10 oz) skinned sea bass fillet, cut into thin strips* ‖ *1½ tablespoons roughly chopped flat leaf parsley* ‖ *extra virgin olive oil, for drizzling (optional)* ‖ *salt*

ONE Bruise the garlic cloves with a large cook's knife (*see page 9*). Heat the olive oil in a large frying pan over a low heat. Stir in the garlic and chillies and cook, stirring occasionally, for 10 minutes. If the garlic begins to colour, simply remove the pan from the hob and let the flavours infuse in the heat of the pan. **TWO** Stir the tomatoes and their juice into the infused oil and pour in the wine. Season lightly with salt, bring to the boil and cook over a medium heat for 12–15 minutes until thickened. **THREE** Meanwhile, cook the pasta in a large saucepan of salted boiling water according to the packet instructions until *al dente*. Drain, reserving a ladleful of the cooking water. When the pasta is almost ready, stir the fish and parsley into the sauce and cook for 2 minutes until the fish turns opaque. **FOUR** Add the drained pasta to the sauce and cook, stirring, for 30 seconds. Add the reserved water and stir until the pasta is well coated in the sauce. Serve immediately with a drizzle of extra virgin olive oil, if you like.

Serves 4

NUTRIENT ANALYSIS PER SERVING 1918 kJ – 450 kcal – 27 g protein – 71 g carbohydrate – 9 g sugars – 7 g fat – 1 g saturates – 7 g fibre – 73 mg sodium

HEALTHY TIP The combination of pasta, low-fat fish and tomatoes makes this a very healthy dish. Fish is an excellent source of protein, pasta adds carbohydrate to complement this and tomatoes are packed with vitamins.

Rigatoni with roasted cherry tomatoes and fennel seeds

These home-roasted tomatoes have all the concentrated flavour of sun-dried tomatoes, but because they have only been half dried, all it takes is a vigorous stir to create a luscious pasta sauce.

INGREDIENTS *500 g (1 lb) cherry tomatoes, halved* ‖ *1½ tablespoons olive oil* ‖ *2 garlic cloves, finely chopped* ‖ *1 tablespoon fennel seeds* ‖ *350 g (11½ oz) dried rigatoni* ‖ *salt*

ONE Arrange the tomatoes, cut side up, in a single layer in a roasting tin lined with greaseproof paper. Drizzle with the oil, then top each tomato half with a little garlic and a few fennel seeds. Season lightly with salt and cook in a preheated oven, 120°C (250°F), Gas Mark ½, for 1 hour. **TWO** Cook the pasta in a large saucepan of salted boiling water according to the packet instructions until *al dente*. Drain, reserving a ladleful of the cooking water, and return the pasta to the pan. **THREE** Add the roasted tomatoes and cook, stirring, for 30 seconds, then add the reserved water and stir until the pasta is well coated in the sauce. Serve immediately with a drizzle of extra virgin olive oil, if you like.

Serves 4

NUTRIENT ANALYSIS PER SERVING 1585 kJ – 374 kcal – 12 g protein – 70 g carbohydrate – 7 g sugars – 7 g fat – 1 g saturates – 6 g fibre – 17 mg sodium

HEALTHY TIP Tomatoes are an excellent source of vitamin C and betacarotene, and therefore may help to prevent various cancers. Using cherry tomatoes increases the fibre content of the dish.

Farfalle with tuna sauce

Good-quality Italian, Spanish and Portuguese canned tuna in olive oil is truly delicious. Try it in this raw pasta sauce – it is ideal for a light supper in summer. To serve this dish as a pasta salad, refresh the cooked pasta in cold running water before adding the remaining ingredients.

INGREDIENTS *125 g (4 oz) can tuna in olive oil* ‖ *2 tablespoons extra virgin olive oil, plus extra to taste (optional)* ‖ *4 tomatoes, roughly chopped* ‖ *50 g (2 oz) pitted black olives, roughly chopped* ‖ *grated rind of 1 lemon* ‖ *2 garlic cloves, crushed* ‖ *2 tablespoons roughly chopped flat leaf parsley* ‖ *350 g (11½ oz) dried farfalle* ‖ *salt*

ONE Drain the tuna and place in a large serving bowl. Break it up with a fork, then stir in the remaining ingredients, except for the pasta. Season with salt, cover and leave to stand for the flavours to infuse for at least 30 minutes (including the pasta's cooking time). **TWO** Meanwhile, cook the pasta in a large saucepan of salted boiling water according to the packet instructions until *al dente*, then drain. Toss into the sauce. Serve immediately with a drizzle of extra virgin olive oil, if you like.

Serves 4

NUTRIENT ANALYSIS PER SERVING 1854 kJ – 438 kcal – 20 g protein – 68 g carbohydrate – 6 g sugars – 12 g fat – 2 g saturates – 6 g fibre – 383 mg sodium

HEALTHY TIP Tuna is a very good source of protein and is fairly low in fat, so the addition of extra olive oil does not make this recipe too high in fat. Olive oil is a good source of monounsaturated fatty acids, which help to increase the ratio of good HDL to bad LDL cholesterol in the blood.

Spring minestrone

What goes into your minestrone really depends on the time of the year during which you are making it. This springtime combination is packed with punchy flavours. During cooler months try replacing the spring vegetables with *cavolo nero* and borlotti beans.

INGREDIENTS *2 tablespoons olive oil ‖ 1 onion, thinly sliced ‖ 2 carrots, cubed ‖ 2 celery sticks, cubed ‖ 2 whole garlic cloves ‖ 1 potato, peeled and diced ‖ 100 g (3½ oz) shelled peas or broad beans ‖ 1 courgette, cubed ‖ 100 g (3½ oz) green beans, cut into 3.5 cm (1½ inch) pieces ‖ 100 g (3½ oz) plum tomatoes, chopped ‖ 1.2 litres (2 pints) shop-bought or homemade Vegetable Stock (see page 18) ‖ 75 g (3 oz) small pasta shapes, such as ditalini ‖ 8 basil leaves, torn ‖ salt and pepper*
TO SERVE *sliced crusty bread ‖ extra virgin olive oil (optional) ‖ freshly grated Parmesan cheese (optional)*

ONE Heat the olive oil in a large, heavy-based saucepan over a low heat. Add the onion, carrots, celery and garlic and cook, stirring occasionally, for 10 minutes. **TWO** Add the potato, peas or broad beans, courgette and green beans and cook, stirring, for 2 minutes. Add the tomatoes, season with salt and pepper and cook for a further 2 minutes. **THREE** Pour in the stock and bring to the boil over a high heat, then reduce the heat and gently simmer for 20 minutes until all the vegetables are very tender. **FOUR** Add the pasta and basil to the soup and cook, stirring frequently, until the pasta is *al dente*. Adjust the seasoning and serve with bread, extra virgin olive oil for drizzling and Parmesan cheese separately for people to help themselves, if they like.

Serves 4–6

NUTRIENT ANALYSIS PER SERVING 923 kJ – 220 kcal – 7 g protein – 35 g carbohydrate – 8 g sugars – 7 g fat – 1 g saturates – 6 g fibre – 28 mg sodium

HEALTHY TIP Packed with vegetables and delicious flavours, this minestrone is also a very good source of vitamins. Carrots are full of carotene – the precursor of vitamin A – and the green vegetables provide other vitamins, particularly folic acid. Vitamins of the B group, including folic acid, are damaged by heat, so do not overcook any green vegetable.

Pumpkin ravioli

This is a great dinner party dish and is surprisingly easy to assemble. Instead of the traditional sage butter sauce, use just a light drizzle of top-quality extra virgin olive oil. Don't be tempted to serve these with tomato sauce, or you will mask the delicate flavour of the pumpkin filling.

INGREDIENTS *1 quantity 2-egg Basic Pasta Dough* (see page 16) ‖ *extra virgin olive oil, for drizzling* ‖ *salt* ‖ *pepper* ‖ *fried sage leaves, to garnish (optional)*

FILLING *550 g (1 lb 2 oz) pumpkin, peeled, deseeded and cut into large chunks* ‖ *1 egg yolk* ‖ *75 g (3 oz) ricotta cheese* ‖ *2 tablespoons freshly grated Parmesan cheese* ‖ *3 tablespoons dried breadcrumbs* ‖ *¼ teaspoon freshly grated nutmeg* ‖ *6 sage leaves, finely chopped* ‖ *salt (optional)*

ONE Spread the pumpkin out on a baking sheet and roast in a preheated oven, 180°C (350°F), Gas Mark 4, for 25–30 minutes or until tender all the way through. Tip the pumpkin into a small saucepan and mash with a fork. Heat in a saucepan over a medium heat, stirring, until the pumpkin begins to stick to the bottom of the pan. This will remove any excess moisture. Leave to cool, then stir in the remaining filling ingredients. Season with salt, if necessary. **TWO** Roll the pasta dough out following the method on page 16. Work on one pasta sheet at a time. Place a heaped teaspoon of filling on the dough every 5 cm (2 inches) until half the sheet is filled. Fold the empty half over the filled half and gently but firmly push down between the spoonfuls of filling, sealing the pasta and ensuring that no air is trapped. Cut into square or round shapes using a pasta or pastry wheel or biscuit cutter. **THREE** Cook the pasta in a large saucepan of salted boiling water for 2–3 minutes until *al dente*, then drain. Drizzle lightly with extra virgin olive oil, season lightly with pepper and serve with the fried sage leaves, if liked.

Serves 6 (makes about 30 ravioli)

NUTRIENT ANALYSIS PER SERVING 887 kJ – 210 kcal – 10 g protein – 31 g carbohydrate – 2 g sugars – 6 g fat – 3 g saturates – 2 g fibre – 108 mg sodium

HEALTHY TIP Pumpkin, like most red or yellow vegetables, is an excellent source of betacarotene. The antioxidant properties of betacarotene are thought to have a role in the prevention of some cancers.

Meat tortellini *in brodo*

A dish that is comforting and wholesome while still being impressive. It takes some effort to make the tortellini, so you may as well go all out and make your own stock too. Alternatively, cook the tortellini in the beautiful broth left over from making *Bollito Misto* with Salsa Verde (*see page 107*).

INGREDIENTS *1 quantity 2-egg Basic Pasta Dough (see page 16)* ‖ semola di grano duro, *for dusting* ‖ *Beef or Chicken Stock (see page 19)* ‖ *salt*

FILLING *1 teaspoon olive oil* ‖ *1 small onion, finely chopped* ‖ *1 garlic clove* ‖ *100 g (3½ oz) minced veal* ‖ *100 g (3½ oz) minced pork* ‖ *50 g (2 oz) prosciutto crudo, roughly chopped* ‖ *1 tablespoon chopped flat leaf parsley* ‖ *4 tablespoons dry white wine* ‖ *2 tablespoons freshly grated Parmesan cheese, plus extra to serve* ‖ *2 tablespoons dried breadcrumbs* ‖ *¼ teaspoon freshly grated nutmeg* ‖ *salt (optional)*

ONE To make the filling, heat the oil in a heavy-based frying pan over a low heat. Add the onion and garlic and cook, stirring frequently, for 6–7 minutes until softened. Add the minced meats and prosciutto and cook over a medium heat, breaking up with a wooden spoon, then stirring frequently, for 10 minutes until the meat is cooked. Add the parsley and wine and cook until all the liquid has evaporated. Leave to cool, then transfer to a food processor or blender with the remaining filling ingredients. Blend to a coarse paste and season with salt, if necessary. **TWO** Roll the pasta dough out following the method on page 16. Cut into 8 cm (3½ inch) squares and place a nutmeg-sized ball of filling into the centre of each square. Brush a little water around the edges of the squares, then fold the dough over the filling to make triangles. Gently but firmly push down around the filling, sealing the pasta and ensuring that no air has been trapped. Bring the corners on the longest edge of the triangles together and pinch tightly to seal. Set aside on a baking sheet lightly dusted with *semola* and cover with a clean tea towel. **THREE** Bring a large saucepan of stock to the boil and season with a little salt. Add the tortellini and cook for 2–3 minutes or until *al dente*. Serve with a scattering of grated Parmesan.

Serves 6 (makes about 30 tortellini)

NUTRIENT ANALYSIS PER SERVING 1046 kJ – 248 kcal – 17 g protein – 29 g carbohydrate – 1 g sugars – 7 g fat – 3 g saturates – 2 g fibre – 295 mg sodium

HEALTHY TIP A good homemade stock adds delicious flavours to many dishes. If using meat or chicken to make stock, allow to cool and remove the fat by skimming and by 'blotting' the surface with kitchen paper.

Tomato and bread soup

Because of its simplicity, this recipe depends on the ripest of tomatoes and extra-aromatic summer basil. Use a peppery extra virgin olive oil to finish off the dish in style.

INGREDIENTS *2 teaspoons olive oil* ‖ *1 small onion, finely chopped* ‖ *2 garlic cloves, crushed* ‖ *1.25 kg (2½ lb) tomatoes, skinned (see page 9) and roughly chopped* ‖ *600 ml (1 pint) Vegetable Stock (see page 18)* ‖ *200 g (7 oz) day-old crusty bread, crust removed* ‖ *15 large basil leaves, torn* ‖ *extra virgin olive oil, for drizzling* ‖ *salt*

ONE Heat the olive oil in a large, heavy-based saucepan over a low heat. Add the onion and cook, stirring occasionally, for 10 minutes until softened and translucent. Add the garlic and cook, stirring, for 1 minute. **TWO** Stir in the tomatoes and their juice and simmer gently for 30 minutes. **THREE** Pour in the stock and bring to the boil, then break the bread into large chunks and stir into the soup until it absorbs the liquid and begins to break down. If the mixture is too thick, add some boiling water. Remove from the heat, stir in the basil and cover with a tight-fitting lid. Leave to cool for at least 30 minutes before serving with a drizzle of extra virgin olive oil. Eat at room temperature or reheat before serving.

Serves 4

NUTRIENT ANALYSIS PER SERVING 885 kJ – 209 kcal – 7 g protein – 36 g carbohydrate – 12 g sugars – 5 g fat – 1 g saturates – 6 g fibre – 294 mg sodium

HEALTHY TIP Onions contain chromium, one of the trace minerals essential for health. Although only very small amounts are required, chromium improves glucose tolerance and insulin balance and may also have a role in decreasing cholesterol and triglyceride levels in the blood.

Grilled polenta with wild mushrooms
Make this dish in autumn, when wild mushrooms are abundant. You can use any combination such as chanterelles, girolles or porcini, then bulk them up with some regular field mushrooms.

INGREDIENTS *900 ml (1½ pints) water* ‖ *225 g (7½ oz) instant polenta* ‖ *olive oil, for brushing* ‖ *salt and pepper*

TOPPING *1 tablespoon olive oil* ‖ *400 g (13 oz) mixed wild mushrooms, sliced if large* ‖ *large pinch of crushed dried red chillies* ‖ *2 sprigs of thyme, leaves stripped* ‖ *2 garlic cloves, roughly chopped* ‖ *2 tablespoons dry vermouth* ‖ *salt*

ONE Bring the measurement water to the boil in a large, heavy-based saucepan and lightly salt. Place the polenta in a jug with a spout and pour into the water in a slow but steady stream, stirring vigorously with a wooden spoon to prevent any lumps from forming. Reduce the heat to a gentle simmer and cook, stirring continuously, for about 5 minutes or until the polenta is thick and comes away from the sides of the pan. Season with pepper and add more salt, if necessary. Pour the polenta on to a large baking sheet and spread it out with a wet palette knife to a thickness of about 2.5 cm (1 inch). Leave to cool. **TWO** To make the topping, heat the oil in a large, heavy-based frying pan over a high heat and add the mushrooms, chillies and thyme. Season lightly with salt and cook until any liquid released from the mushrooms has evaporated. Add the garlic and vermouth and leave to cook for 1 minute. **THREE** Cut the polenta into evenly sized wedges and brush lightly with oil. Heat a griddle pan until searing hot and griddle the polenta for about 2 minutes on each side. Serve topped with the mixed mushrooms.

Serves 4

NUTRIENT ANALYSIS PER SERVING 1050 kJ – 250 kcal – 7 g protein – 45 g carbohydrate – 1 g sugars – 4 g fat – 1 g saturates – 2 g fibre – 7 mg sodium

HEALTHY TIP Mushrooms contain useful amounts of several B vitamins, which in this dish help to supplement the polenta. Mushrooms also contain copper, an essential trace mineral which is necessary for the development and repair of connective tissue.

Polenta with Parma ham, asparagus and fontina

This dish is great for a quick lunch or light supper. The mild fontina cheese becomes wonderfully oozy and the Parma ham crisps up beautifully under the grill. Delicious!

INGREDIENTS *900 ml (1½ pints) water* ‖ *225 g (7½ oz) instant polenta* ‖ *250 g (8 oz) asparagus, trimmed* ‖ *6 slices of Parma ham* ‖ *100 g (3½ oz) fontina cheese, sliced* ‖ *1 tablespoon freshly grated Parmesan cheese* ‖ *salt and pepper*

ONE Bring the measurement water to the boil in a large, heavy-based saucepan and lightly salt. Place the polenta in a jug with a spout and pour into the water in a slow but steady stream, stirring vigorously with a wooden spoon to prevent any lumps forming. Reduce the heat to a gentle simmer and cook, stirring continuously, for about 5 minutes or until the polenta is thick and comes away from the sides of the pan. Season with pepper and add more salt, if necessary. **TWO** Pour the polenta into a baking dish about 25 x 17 cm (10 x 6½ inches). Blanch the asparagus in a saucepan of boiling water for 1–2 minutes or until just tender. Drain. Top the polenta with a layer of ham, then the asparagus and lastly a layer of fontina and Parmesan. Cook under a preheated very hot grill, about 7 cm (3 inches) from the heat, until crisp and golden. Cut into wedges and serve immediately.

Serves 4 as a primo piatto *or 6 as part of an* antipasto *selection*

NUTRIENT ANALYSIS PER SERVING 1596 kJ – 380 kcal – 21 g protein – 45 g carbohydrate – 2 g sugars – 12 g fat – 6 g saturates – 1 g fibre – 723 mg sodium

HEALTHY TIP Polenta is made from maize, which has a high content of nicotinic acid, one of the B-group vitamins. In maize the vitamin is in an unavailable form, but if combined with a dairy product (such as the cheese in this dish) the nicotinic acid can be used by the body.

Lemony prawn and pea risotto

If you want to wow your guests, serve this dish at a dinner party followed by Monkfish Skewers Wrapped in Prosciutto (*see page 78*).

INGREDIENTS *12 uncooked large king prawns* ‖ *900 ml (1½ pints) shop-bought or homemade Fish Stock (see page 19)* ‖ *1 tablespoon olive oil* ‖ *1 small fennel bulb, finely chopped* ‖ *275 g (9 oz) vialone nano, arborio or carnaroli rice* ‖ *150 ml (¼ pint) dry vermouth* ‖ *75 g (3 oz) shelled fresh or frozen peas* ‖ *finely grated rind of 1 lemon* ‖ *1 tablespoon extra virgin olive oil* ‖ *1 teaspoon olive oil* ‖ *1 garlic clove, chopped* ‖ *juice of ½ lemon*

ONE Peel and devein the prawns (*see page 9*), leaving tails on. Return to the refrigerator and place the shells in a saucepan with the stock. Bring to the boil, then reduce the heat and simmer, uncovered, for 20 minutes. Strain the stock into a measuring jug, add enough water to make 900 ml (1½ pints) and return to the pan. Bring to the boil, then reduce the heat to a gentle simmer. **TWO** Heat the olive oil in a heavy-based saucepan over a low heat. Add the fennel and cook, stirring occasionally, for 10 minutes until softened. Add the rice and cook, stirring, for 1 minute. Pour in the vermouth and cook, stirring, until all the liquid has been absorbed. **THREE** Add 2 ladlefuls of hot stock and adjust the heat to a gentle simmer. Stir continuously until the stock has been absorbed and the rice parts when a wooden spoon is run through it. Add another ladleful of stock and continue stirring and adding stock in stages until the rice is creamy and tender to the bite, adding the peas with the last ladleful of stock. This will take about 18–20 minutes. **FOUR** Remove from the heat, add the grated lemon rind and extra virgin olive oil and stir vigorously for 15 seconds. Cover and leave to stand for 1 minute. **FIVE** When the risotto is almost ready, cook the prawns; heat a large frying pan over a high heat and coat with the oil. Add the prawns and garlic and cook, stirring, for 2 minutes until the prawns turn pink. Stir into the risotto with the lemon juice and serve immediately.

Serves 4

NUTRIENT ANALYSIS PER SERVING 1659 kJ – 393 kcal – 11 g protein – 65 g carbohydrate – 3 g sugars – 8 g fat – 1 g saturates – 2 g fibre – 63 mg sodium

HEALTHY TIP Like all shellfish prawns contain cholesterol. Although dietary cholesterol is less important than total fat intake for control of blood cholesterol, it is sensible to limit quantities of shellfish eaten.

Courgette flower risotto

To cut down on the saturated fats, the butter used in classic risotto recipes has been replaced with olive oil in this book. The result is a fresher and lighter risotto, which, if you stir religiously while cooking, will be just as creamy as you would expect.

INGREDIENTS *900 ml (1½ pints) shop-bought or homemade Vegetable Stock (see page 18)* ‖ *1 tablespoon olive oil* ‖ *1 onion, finely chopped* ‖ *1 garlic clove, finely chopped* ‖ *275 g (9 oz) vialone nano, arborio or carnaroli rice* ‖ *150 ml (¼ pint) dry white wine* ‖ *2 large courgettes* ‖ *4 courgette flowers, cut into 2.5 cm (1 inch) strips* ‖ *grated rind of ½ lemon* ‖ *1½ tablespoons freshly grated Parmesan cheese* ‖ *1 tablespoon extra virgin olive oil* ‖ *pepper*

ONE Bring the stock to the boil in a saucepan, then reduce the heat to a gentle simmer. **TWO** Heat the olive oil in a heavy-based saucepan over a low heat. Add the onion and cook, stirring occasionally, for 10 minutes until softened. Add the garlic and rice and cook, stirring, for 1 minute. Pour in the wine and cook, stirring, until the liquid has been absorbed. **THREE** Add 2 ladlefuls of hot stock and adjust the heat to a gentle simmer. Stir continuously until the stock has been absorbed and the rice parts when a wooden spoon is run through it. Thinly slice one of the courgettes and stir into the pan. Add another ladleful of stock and continue stirring and adding stock in stages until the rice is creamy and almost tender to the bite. This will take about 16–18 minutes. **FOUR** Coarsely grate the remaining courgette and stir into the pan with the courgette flowers. Add a final ladleful of stock and cook, stirring, for 1 minute. The rice should now be tender, but still firm. **FIVE** Remove from the heat and stir in the lemon rind, Parmesan and extra virgin olive oil. Stir vigorously for 15 seconds, then cover with a tight-fitting lid and leave to stand for 1 minute. Season with pepper and serve immediately.

Serves 4

NUTRIENT ANALYSIS PER SERVING 1444 kJ – 340 kcal – 8 g protein – 65 g carbohydrate – 1 g sugars – 5 g fat – 1 g saturates – 2 g fibre – 48 mg sodium

HEALTHY TIP This risotto has a low fat content and the addition of courgettes and onions provides good sources of vitamins and minerals. Go easy on the added Parmesan to keep the fat content low.

Secondi piatti –
fish and seafood

Roasted sea bass with potatoes and wild mushrooms

This all-in-one dish makes an impressive, hassle-free main course for a dinner party. If fresh wild mushrooms are not available, use a combination of dried porcini and cultivated mushrooms, reducing the soaking liquid from the porcini and adding it to the potatoes with the mushrooms, to intensify the wild mushroom flavour.

INGREDIENTS *875 g (1¾ lb) potatoes, peeled* ‖ *2 garlic cloves, thinly sliced* ‖ *3 tablespoons olive oil* ‖ *250 g (8 oz) mixed wild mushrooms, sliced if large* ‖ *4 sea bass fillets, about 175 g (6 oz) each* ‖ *½ tablespoon chopped flat leaf parsley* ‖ *extra virgin olive oil, for drizzling* ‖ *salt and pepper*

ONE Slice the potatoes about 1 cm (½ inch) thick and place in a large roasting tin lined with greaseproof paper. Stir in half the garlic and 2 tablespoons of the olive oil and season with salt and pepper. Spread the potatoes out in a single layer, then roast in a preheated oven, 240°C (475°F), Gas Mark 9, for 18–20 minutes or until cooked through and golden. **TWO** Meanwhile, heat ½ tablespoon of the remaining olive oil in a frying pan over a high heat, add the mushrooms and the remaining garlic and cook, stirring frequently, until just tender. Season with salt and pepper. **THREE** Stir the cooked mushrooms into the roasted potatoes. Season the sea bass fillets, then sit them on top of the potatoes, skin side up. Scatter with the parsley and drizzle the fish with the remaining olive oil. Roast for 10–12 minutes until the fish is cooked through. Serve immediately with a drizzle of extra virgin olive oil.

Serves 4

NUTRIENT ANALYSIS PER SERVING 1839 kJ – 438 kcal – 40 g protein – 38 g carbohydrate – 2 g sugars – 15 g fat – 2 g saturates – 5 g fibre – 140 mg sodium

HEALTHY TIP Sea bass is a low-fat fish that is an excellent source of protein and provides useful amounts of vitamin A and selenium. Selenium is thought to prevent the formation of free radicals and thus aid prevention of cancer.

Sea bass *al cartoccio* with tomatoes and fennel

Roasting *al cartoccio* or 'in the bag', where the ingredients are sealed in a foil or greaseproof paper parcel to steam, is a great low-fat cooking technique. You can replace the sea bass with sea bream or, for ease of serving, use fillets instead of whole fish. Great accompaniments are simple boiled potatoes, Broccoli with Garlic and Chilli (*see page 113*) or Green Beans with Lemon and Garlic (*see page 121*).

INGREDIENTS *16 cherry tomatoes* ‖ *1 large fennel bulb, very finely sliced* ‖ *2 tablespoons lemon juice* ‖ *1 garlic clove, finely chopped* ‖ *1 sea bass, about 1.25 kg (2½ lb), cleaned and scaled* ‖ *1 tablespoon olive oil* ‖ *salt and pepper*

ONE Place the tomatoes in a bowl and crush them between your hands until they have all burst. **TWO** Cut a piece of foil or greaseproof paper 4 times the length of the sea bass and fold it in half to give you double thickness. Mix the fennel with the lemon juice and garlic. Place half the fennel mixture in the centre of the sheet, more or less in the shape of the sea bass. **THREE** Using your hands, rub the oil into the sea bass all over, then season the fish with salt and pepper and sit it on the fennel. Slash the skin of the fish 3 or 4 times on both sides to allow the flavours to infuse. **FOUR** Place a few slices of the remaining fennel inside the sea bass and scatter the remainder over the top. Add the tomatoes and their juice, then bring the edges of the paper together to make a loose parcel. Seal the edges by folding tightly, then place the parcel on a baking sheet. Cook in a preheated oven, 220°C (425°F), Gas Mark 7, for 18–20 minutes. Transfer the parcel to a serving platter and leave to stand for 5 minutes. Split the parcel open at the table to share the wonderful aroma.

Serves 4

NUTRIENT ANALYSIS PER SERVING 998 kJ – 237 kcal – 38 g protein – 4 g carbohydrate – 4 g sugars – 8 g fat – 1 g saturates – 1 g fibre – 146 mg sodium

HEALTHY TIP Adding tomatoes and fennel to the sea bass boosts the vitamin and mineral content in this low-fat dish. Sea bass provides useful amounts of pantothenic acid (essential for growth and reproduction) and other vitamins of the B group.

Sea bream in *acquapazza*

Poaching fish in *acquapazza*, or crazy water, is a quick and easy way of cooking fish while making a healthy, flavoursome sauce for it at the same time. Feel free to use sea bass, brill or monkfish instead of sea bream. The important thing is that it should be super fresh! Serve with a side salad or green vegetables.

INGREDIENTS *2 teaspoons olive oil* ‖ *1 small onion, finely sliced* ‖ *2 garlic cloves, crushed* ‖ *3 tomatoes, deseeded and cubed* ‖ *400 ml (14 fl oz) water* ‖ *1 tablespoon roughly chopped flat leaf parsley* ‖ *2 sea bream, about 625 g (1¼ lb) each, cleaned and scaled* ‖ *salt*

ONE Heat the oil in a large, shallow saucepan over a low heat. Add the onion and cook, stirring occasionally, for 6–7 minutes, then stir in the garlic, tomatoes and measurement water. Increase the heat to bring to the boil, then stir in the parsley. Reduce the heat to a gentle simmer and season with salt. **TWO** Add the sea bream to the pan and cook in the gently simmering broth for 6–8 minutes on each side. Remove the fish from the pan and strain the cooking liquid. Return the liquid to the pan and reduce slightly over a high heat. Meanwhile, remove the fish from the bone. **THREE** Place the sea bream fillets on to 4 plates. Adjust the seasoning of the cooking liquid and spoon a couple of tablespoons over each fillet. Serve immediately.

Serves 4

NUTRIENT ANALYSIS PER SERVING 857 kJ – 204 kcal – 34 g protein – 2 g carbohydrate – 1 g sugars – 7 g fat – 0 g saturates – 0 g fibre – 210 mg sodium

HEALTHY TIP White fish such as monkfish, cod and haddock have a very low fat content, whereas fatty fishes such as mackerel, herring and salmon contain quite large amounts of oils which are high in the omega-3 fatty acids thought to protect health. In between are the more delicate white fish such as mullet and bream which do contain some fat, but much less than the 'fatty' fish. All fish is a very good source of protein.

Stuffed squid with herbs and anchovies

You will often find Italian dishes where squid are stuffed with rice. Although delicious, the result can be quite heavy, not to say time-consuming to make. Here, the squid is stuffed with a flavoursome breadcrumb mixture for a quick, light main course. Serve with a green salad or the Peperonata (*see page 123*).

INGREDIENTS *8 squid, about 625 g (1¼ lb) total weight, cleaned* (see page 9) ‖ *2 teaspoons olive oil* ‖ *125 ml (4 fl oz) dry white wine*

FILLING *1 teaspoon olive oil* ‖ *1 small onion, finely chopped* ‖ *large pinch of crushed dried red chillies* ‖ *4 anchovy fillets in salt or olive oil, well-rinsed or drained and roughly chopped* ‖ *2 garlic cloves, crushed* ‖ *150 g (5 oz) fresh white breadcrumbs* ‖ *1 tablespoon roughly chopped mint* ‖ *2 tablespoons roughly chopped flat leaf parsley* ‖ *grated rind of 1 lemon* ‖ *salt (optional)*

ONE Pull the 'wings' of the squid – the flat pieces of flesh attached to either side of the body – away from the body and roughly chop. Roughly chop the tentacles and set all the squid aside. **TWO** To make the filling, heat the oil in a frying pan over a low heat. Add the onion and chillies and cook, stirring occasionally, for 10 minutes until the onions are softened and translucent. Stir in the chopped squid, anchovies and garlic and cook over a high heat, stirring, for 1 minute. Leave to cool, then stir in the remaining filling ingredients. **THREE** Stuff the squid body cavities three-quarters full with the filling, using a teaspoon to help push the filling in. Secure the ends closed with cocktail sticks. **FOUR** Heat the oil in a large, heavy-based frying pan over a high heat and cook the squid for 1–2 minutes on each side, then pour in the wine and boil for 1 minute, carefully turning the squid in the sauce. Serve immediately.

Serves 4

NUTRIENT ANALYSIS PER SERVING 1111 kJ – 264 kcal – 28 g protein – 22 g carbohydrate – 2 g sugars – 5 g fat – 1 g saturates – 2 g fibre – 590 mg sodium

HEALTHY TIP Squid is fairly low in fat. The addition of anchovies to this dish provides some omega-3 fatty acids, and the healthy effect of these is enhanced by the addition of garlic, which helps prevent the formation of blood clots.

Mixed seafood grill

This impressive seafood feast is perfect shared *al fresco* between friends. Weather allowing, it can be cooked on the barbecue rather than griddled. Serve with salads, such as the Panzanella (*see page 36*) and the Fennel, Orange and Olive Salad (*see page 34*).

INGREDIENTS *12 uncooked large king prawns, unpeeled but deveined* (see page 9) ‖ *300 g (10 oz) squid, cleaned* (see page 9*), cut into 3 cm squares, and inside flesh lightly scored in a crisscross pattern* ‖ *12 live clams, cleaned* (see page 9*)* ‖ *12 live mussels, cleaned* (see page 9*)*
TO SERVE *lemon wedges* ‖ *crusty bread (optional)*
DRESSING *1 garlic clove, peeled but kept whole* ‖ *3 tablespoons extra virgin olive oil* ‖ *1 tablespoon chopped flat leaf parsley*

ONE To make the dressing, bruise the garlic clove with a large cook's knife (*see page 9*). Place in a bowl with the oil and parsley. Leave to infuse for at least 20 minutes. **TWO** Heat a ridged cast-iron griddle pan over a high heat until it is searing hot, or if barbecuing, get the coals to the stage where there are no more flames and the coals are covered with a thin layer of grey ash. Lightly brush the prawns and squid with the dressing, add to the pan or barbecue and cook for 1–2 minutes on each side until charred. Transfer to a serving platter. Add the clams and mussels to the pan or barbecue and cook until they open – this should take 4–5 minutes. Add them to the platter, then drizzle all the seafood with the remaining dressing. Serve immediately with lemon wedges and bread on the side, if you like.

Serves 4

NUTRIENT ANALYSIS PER SERVING 757 kJ – 182 kcal – 21 g protein – 2 g carbohydrate – 0 g sugars – 10 g fat – 1 g saturates – 0 g fibre – 355 mg sodium

HEALTHY TIP Most of the fat in this recipe comes from the oil in the dressing – only a small amount comes from the fish. Olive oil is high in calories, like all oils, but has a high proportion of monounsaturated fatty acids, which help to maintain the best ratio of good HDL to bad LDL cholesterol in the blood.

Grilled red mullet with thyme and lemon

The most common way of cooking fish in summer is simply to grill it with some fresh herbs or even just seasoned with salt and a drizzle of olive oil. Use this technique for any whole round fish, such as mackerel, trout or sea bass. Serve with a salad or green vegetables.

INGREDIENTS *4 red mullet, cleaned and scaled* ‖ *1 tablespoon olive oil* ‖ *2 tablespoons roughly chopped thyme leaves* ‖ *2 garlic cloves, finely chopped* ‖ *1 lemon* ‖ *salt and pepper*

ONE Pat the fish dry with kitchen paper. Cut 2–3 deep slashes across the width of both sides of each mullet, then brush all over the fish with the oil. Season with salt and pepper. **TWO** Combine the chopped thyme and garlic, then rub into the body cavities of the fish and the slashes. Cut the lemon in half lengthways, then thinly slice each half. Place a lemon slice in each slash, then place a couple of slices inside each fish. **THREE** Place the fish on a nonstick baking sheet and cook under a preheated very hot grill, about 10 cm (4 inches) from the heat, until the skin is beginning to char, then turn the fish over to char the other side.

Serves 4

NUTRIENT ANALYSIS PER SERVING 500 kJ – 120 kcal – 16 g protein – 1 g carbohydrate – 0 g sugars – 6 g fat – 0 g saturates – 0 g fibre – 83 mg sodium

HEALTHY TIP Mullet contains a moderate amount of fat, similar to the amount found in trout, so it supplies a certain amount of omega-3 fatty acids. It is also a useful source of trace minerals and vitamins of the B group.

Octopus stew

Octopus is popular in Italy, but cooks who have never handled it before often shy away from it. Granted, it can be awkward to clean, so ask your fishmonger to do it for you. Octopus needs long, slow cooking – be patient and it will reward you with the tenderest, melt-in-the-mouth results.

INGREDIENTS *1 octopus, about 750 g (1½ lb), cleaned* ‖ *1½ tablespoons olive oil* ‖ *3 garlic cloves, peeled but kept whole* ‖ *1 small onion, finely chopped* ‖ *large pinch of crushed dried red chillies* ‖ *500 ml (17 fl oz) dry white wine* ‖ *400 g (13 oz) can plum tomatoes, drained and roughly chopped* ‖ *1 tablespoon tomato purée* ‖ *75 g (3 oz) shelled fresh or frozen peas* ‖ *2 tablespoons roughly chopped parsley* ‖ *extra virgin olive oil, for drizzling (optional)* ‖ *salt and pepper (optional)* ‖ *crusty bread, to serve*

ONE Place the octopus in a flameproof casserole pan with a tight-fitting lid and pour in half the olive oil. Bruise 2 garlic cloves (*see page 9*), add to the pan and cover. Cook over a very low heat for 2–2½ hours or until the thickest part of the octopus can be easily pierced with a fork. **TWO** Meanwhile, heat the remaining olive oil in a large, heavy-based frying pan over a low heat. Add the onion and cook, stirring occasionally, for 10 minutes until softened and translucent. Chop the remaining garlic, add to the pan with the chillies and cook, stirring, for 1 minute. Pour in the wine, increase the heat and boil for 1 minute. Add the tomatoes and tomato purée and boil until the sauce has reduced by half. **THREE** Once the octopus is tender, lift it from the dish and cut it into 7 cm (3 inch) pieces. It will have released quite a lot of liquid while cooking. Return the pan with this liquid to the hob and add the sauce. Boil until reduced by one-third, then stir in the octopus. Reduce the heat to a very gentle simmer and cook, uncovered, for a further 20 minutes. Add the peas and parsley and adjust the seasoning, if necessary. **FOUR** Cover and leave the stew to stand off the heat for 10 minutes. Serve with a drizzle of extra virgin olive oil, if you like, and some bread to mop up the sauce.

Serves 4

NUTRIENT ANALYSIS PER SERVING 1220 kJ – 290 kcal – 29 g protein – 8 g carbohydrate – 6 g sugars – 7 g fat – 1 g saturates – 2 g fibre – 60 mg sodium

HEALTHY TIP The tomatoes and tomato purée in this low-fat dish provide a good source of lycopene which may help to protect against cancers of the bladder and pancreas.

Monkfish skewers wrapped in prosciutto

These little skewers are perfectly designed. The prosciutto flavours the monkfish, while protecting it from the fierce heat, so the fish remains moist and tender. They are gorgeous served on a hot summer's day with the Baked Tomatoes with Breadcrumbs (*see page 117*).

INGREDIENTS *750 g (1½ lb) monkfish tail, boned and skinned* ‖ *6 slices of prosciutto crudo* ‖ *½ tablespoon roughly chopped rosemary leaves* ‖ *½ tablespoon olive oil* ‖ *lemon wedges, to serve*

ONE If using wooden skewers, soak 4 in cold water for at least 1 hour. Cut the monkfish into 12 pieces about 2.5 cm (1 inch) each. Cut the prosciutto slices lengthways to make 12 strips. **TWO** Lay the prosciutto strips side by side on a work surface. Scatter with the rosemary, then place a piece of fish at the bottom of each prosciutto strip and roll up to wrap the fish. Thread 3 pieces of wrapped fish on to each skewer and brush with the oil. **THREE** Place the skewers on a rack over a baking sheet and cook under a preheated very hot grill, about 7 cm (3 inches) from the heat, for 6–7 minutes, turning the skewers over halfway through. Serve immediately.

Serves 4

NUTRIENT ANALYSIS PER SERVING 825 kJ – 195 kcal – 35 g protein – 0 g carbohydrate – 0 g sugars – 6 g fat – 2 g saturates – 0 g fibre – 704 mg sodium

HEALTHY TIP Monkfish is very low in fat and contains useful amounts of vitamins of the B group, as well as some trace minerals, such as copper and selenium.

Swordfish with lemon, olives and capers

Swordfish has a meaty texture that benefits from quick searing so that the flesh retains its juiciness. The flavoursome topping is a favourite in Sicily and is just as delicious scattered over griddled tuna, chicken breast or steak. Serve the dish with salad or green vegetables.

INGREDIENTS *1 tablespoon olive oil* ‖ *2 tablespoons lemon juice* ‖ *½ red chilli, deseeded and chopped* ‖ *4 swordfish steaks, about 175 g (6 oz) each* ‖ *rind of 1 lemon, roughly chopped* ‖ *1 garlic clove, roughly chopped* ‖ *2½ tablespoons capers, soaked, drained and roughly chopped* ‖ *10 pitted black olives, roughly chopped* ‖ *1 tablespoon roughly chopped mint* ‖ *extra virgin olive oil, for drizzling (optional)* ‖ *salt*

ONE Combine the olive oil, lemon juice and chilli in a large, shallow non-reactive dish. Add the swordfish steaks and turn in the marinade so that they are coated on both sides, then cover and leave to marinate for 15 minutes. **TWO** Meanwhile, make the topping by combining the lemon rind, garlic, capers, olives and mint. **THREE** To cook the swordfish, heat a ridged cast-iron griddle pan over a high heat until it is searing hot. Lightly season the steaks with salt, add to the pan and cook for 2–3 minutes on each side so that they are just cooked through. Serve with a scattering of the topping and, if you like, a light drizzling of extra virgin olive oil.

Serves 4

NUTRIENT ANALYSIS PER SERVING 976 kJ – 233 kcal – 32 g protein – 0 g carbohydrate – 0 g sugars – 12 g fat – 2 g saturates – 1 g fibre – 617 mg sodium

HEALTHY TIP Swordfish contains a moderate amount of fat, but is an excellent source of protein. The lemony topping in this dish is a good source of vitamin C and the garlic, olives and mint provide some useful trace minerals.

Ligurian seafood stew

This vibrant one-pot meal depends on the freshest fish for its success. Grill some bread to place at the base of your dish, if you like, then spoon over the lovely stew.

INGREDIENTS *1½ tablespoons olive oil* ‖ *1 small onion, finely chopped* ‖ *1 small fennel bulb, finely chopped* ‖ *1 garlic clove, finely chopped* ‖ *12 live clams, cleaned* (see **page 9**) ‖ *12 live mussels, cleaned* (see **page 9**) ‖ *300 ml (½ pint) dry white wine* ‖ *400 g (13 oz) tomatoes, skinned* (see **page 9**) *and roughly chopped* ‖ *275 g (9 oz) squid, cleaned* (see **page 9**) *and cut into 2.5 cm (1 inch) rings* ‖ *275 g (9 oz) chunky white fish fillets, such as monkfish, halibut, turbot or cod* ‖ *275 g (9 oz) delicate white fish fillets, such as red mullet, red snapper, sea bass or sea bream* ‖ *8 uncooked king prawns, deveined but kept in their shells* (see **page 9**) ‖ *extra virgin olive oil, for drizzling (optional)* ‖ *salt*

ONE Heat the oil in a large, heavy-based saucepan over a low heat. Add the onion and fennel and cook, stirring occasionally, for 8 minutes. Add the garlic and cook, stirring, for 1 minute. Increase the heat to medium, stir in the clams and mussels and cook, covered, for 4–5 minutes until the shells have opened. Remove the shellfish from the pan with a slotted spoon, leaving the vegetables in the pan, and transfer to a sieve set over a bowl. Return the collected juices to the pan. **TWO** Add the wine and boil vigorously for 1 minute, then add the tomatoes and their juice and season lightly with salt. Bring to the boil, then reduce the heat to a gentle simmer and cook, uncovered, for 20 minutes. Add the squid and cook for a further 10 minutes. **THREE** Cut all the fish into pieces about 6 cm (2½ inches) long. Add the chunky fish to the pan and simmer gently for 2–3 minutes, then add the delicate fish and cook for 2–3 minutes before stirring in the prawns. **FOUR** Return the clams and mussels to the pan. Cover and leave to stand off the heat for 5 minutes. Serve with a drizzle of extra virgin olive oil, if you like.

Serves 4

NUTRIENT ANALYSIS PER SERVING 1380 kJ – 329 kcal – 45 g protein – 7 g carbohydrate – 5 g sugars – 8 g fat – 1 g saturates – 2 g fibre – 380 mg sodium

HEALTHY TIP Fish is an excellent source of protein and contains useful amounts of the B-group vitamins, some selenium and small amounts of trace minerals.

Stuffed tuna rolls with white wine
Stuffed with a pine nut, raisin and breadcrumb filling, these tuna rolls are surprisingly light. Make sure you brown them thoroughly in the pan, as the caramelized juices are what give the wine sauce its depth of flavour. Serve with a green vegetable or the Peperonata (*see page 122*).

INGREDIENTS *4 fresh tuna steaks, about 125 g (4 oz) each* ‖ *2 teaspoons olive oil* ‖ *125 ml (4 fl oz) dry white wine* ‖ *2 tablespoons roughly chopped flat leaf parsley* ‖ *salt*

FILLING *2 teaspoons olive oil* ‖ *1 fennel bulb, finely chopped* ‖ *1 tablespoon pine nuts* ‖ *1 tablespoon raisins* ‖ *1 garlic clove, crushed* ‖ *75 g (3 oz) fresh breadcrumbs*

ONE To make the filling, heat the oil in a frying pan over a low heat. Add the fennel and cook, stirring occasionally, for 10 minutes. Add the pine nuts, raisins and garlic and cook, stirring, for 1–2 minutes until the pine nuts begin to colour, then remove from the heat and stir in the breadcrumbs. Leave to cool. **TWO** Lay the tuna steaks in a single layer on a work surface and cover with clingfilm. Beat with a meat mallet or rolling pin until they are as thin as possible without them breaking. Remove the clingfilm and season lightly with salt. **THREE** Take a quarter of the filling and squeeze it between your fingers to bind it together. Form it into a sausage shape, then place it along a short edge of a tuna steak. Roll up the tuna and secure it with a cocktail stick. Repeat with the remaining tuna steaks. **FOUR** Heat the oil in a large frying pan over a high heat, add the tuna rolls and cook, turning frequently, for 3–4 minutes until coloured on all sides. Pour in the wine and cook until it has reduced by half, then scatter with the parsley. Serve immediately.

Serves 4

NUTRIENT ANALYSIS PER SERVING 1320 kJ – 314 kcal – 34 g protein – 16 g carbohydrate – 7 g sugars – 12 g fat – 2 g saturates – 1 g fibre – 167 mg sodium

HEALTHY TIP Raisins are a concentrated source of some useful nutrients. They provide a good source of iron, are high in potassium, provide useful amounts of many vitamins and have a high fibre content.

Salt cod with chickpeas
As they cook, the chickpeas absorb the flavour of the herbs and chilli, then the cod benefits from soaking in the same broth. As for the salt in salt cod, don't worry – the majority will be gone before you start cooking the fish. Serve it spooned over grilled crusty bread.

INGREDIENTS *625 g (1¼ lb) thick salt cod fillets, cut into 10 cm (4 inch) pieces* ‖ *250 g (8 oz) dried chickpeas* ‖ *3 garlic cloves, peeled but kept whole* ‖ *1 red chilli, halved lengthways* ‖ *1 bay leaf* ‖ *3 parsley stalks* ‖ *1 sprig of rosemary* ‖ *2 tablespoons roughly chopped flat leaf parsley* ‖ *finely grated rind of 1 lemon* ‖ *extra virgin olive oil, for drizzling (optional)* ‖ *salt (optional) and pepper*

ONE Soak the salt cod in a bowl of cold water for 48 hours, changing the water 5–6 times a day – the larger the bowl you soak the cod in, the less obsessive you need to be about this. Soak the chickpeas overnight in cold water. **TWO** Drain and rinse the chickpeas, then place them in a large saucepan. Add enough cold water to cover by about 7 cm (3 inches) and bring to the boil over a high heat. Skim off any scum that rises to the surface, then reduce the heat to a gentle simmer. Add 2 garlic cloves and the chilli. Tie the bay leaf, parsley stalks and rosemary together with a length of clean string and add to the pan. Cook the chickpeas, uncovered, for 1½–2 hours until tender. Remove and discard the herbs. **THREE** When the chickpeas are almost ready, drain the cod, plunge into a large saucepan of boiling water and simmer for 6–7 minutes. Drain and, when cool enough to handle, break into large flakes, removing and discarding the skin and any bones. **FOUR** Gently stir the cod into the chickpea broth and simmer for 1 minute. Crush the remaining garlic and stir it into the pan with the parsley and lemon rind. Season with pepper and, if necessary, salt. Cover and leave to stand off the heat for 10 minutes. Serve, drizzled with extra virgin olive oil, if you like.

Serves 4

NUTRIENT ANALYSIS PER SERVING 1714 kJ – 407 kcal – 59 g protein – 32 g carbohydrate – 2 g sugars – 5 g fat – 0 g saturates – 9 g fibre – 146 mg sodium

HEALTHY TIP There may still be some salt left in the cod after soaking, so do taste the dish before adding any more salt. If you use canned chickpeas instead of dried try to use those canned in water, not brine.

Secondi piatti –
meat and poultry

Grilled spatchcocked chicken with chilli

This recipe is known as *Pollo alla diavola* (chicken devil-style), but opinions vary as to whether this is in reference to the fiery marinade or the tradition of cooking it over an open fire. This version is cooked under the grill, but the same method can be used for barbecuing.

INGREDIENTS *1 organic or free-range chicken, about 1 kg (2 lb) ‖ 2 tablespoons olive oil ‖ juice of 1 lemon ‖ 1½ teaspoons dried red chilli flakes ‖ salt ‖ lemon wedges, to serve*

ONE To spatchcock the chicken, remove the backbone by cutting down either side of it with poultry shears or kitchen scissors. Open the chicken up with your hands and lay it, skin side up, on a chopping board. Flatten the bird by pressing firmly along the breastbone with the heel of your hand, breaking the breastbone. **TWO** Combine the oil, lemon juice and chilli flakes in a shallow, non-reactive dish and add the chicken. Cover and leave to marinate in the refrigerator for at least 2 hours or overnight, turning it once or twice. **THREE** Remove the chicken from the marinade and season with salt. Place on a rack over a baking sheet, skin side down, and cook under a preheated very hot grill, about 10 cm (4 inches) from the heat, for 15 minutes, basting once. Turn the chicken skin side up and cook for a further 12–15 minutes, basting from time to time, until the chicken is golden and the juices run clear when the thigh is pierced with a knife. Serve with plenty of lemon wedges.

Serves 4

NUTRIENT ANALYSIS PER SERVING 1100 kJ – 264 kcal – 30 g protein – 0 g carbohydrate – 0 g sugars – 16 g fat – 4 g saturates – 0 g fibre – 87 mg sodium

HEALTHY TIP Olive oil contains high levels of vitamin E, making it a powerful weapon in the fight against disease and ageing. There is increasing evidence that consumption of olive oil is linked to a longer and healthier life, as Italians who use it regularly have a much better health record than those in countries where animal fats are used instead.

Roast chicken with rosemary

Nothing could be simpler than this family staple. Like all good Italian cooking, the flavours are kept simple, letting the fresh ingredients speak for themselves. Serve it with Green Beans with Lemon and Garlic (*see page 121*), Fresh Peas with Prosciutto (*see page 126*) or Baked Tomatoes with Breadcrumbs (*see page 117*).

INGREDIENTS *4 garlic cloves, peeled but kept whole* ‖ *4 sprigs of rosemary* ‖ *1 organic or free-range chicken, about 1.75 kg (3½ lb)* ‖ *2 teaspoons olive oil* ‖ *salt and pepper*

ONE Place the garlic cloves and 3 rosemary sprigs in the body cavity of the chicken. **TWO** Pat the chicken skin dry with kitchen paper and rub the oil all over the outside of the bird. Strip the leaves off the remaining rosemary sprig and rub over the bird, with a little salt and pepper. **THREE** Place the chicken, breast side up, in a roasting tin and roast in a preheated oven, 220°C (425°F), Gas Mark 7, for 10 minutes. Turn the chicken breast side down, reduce the oven temperature to 180°C (350°F), Gas Mark 4, and roast for a further 20 minutes. Finally, turn the chicken back to its original position and roast for a further 25 minutes until the skin is crisp and golden and the juices run clear when the thigh is pierced with a knife. If there is any sign of pink, cook for a further 10 minutes. Transfer to a serving plate and leave for 5 minutes for the juices to settle before serving with the pan juices.

Serves 4

NUTRIENT ANALYSIS PER SERVING 1790 kJ – 430 kcal – 50 g protein – 0 g carbohydrate – 0 g sugars – 25 g fat – 7 g saturates – 0 g fibre – 150 mg sodium

HEALTHY TIP Most of the fat in chicken is in the skin. Roasting until the skin is crisp reduces the fat content, but take care to skim as much of the fat as possible off the pan juices. Blotting the top of the juice with kitchen paper is a useful way of getting rid of more fat.

Veal escalopes with basil

These fragrant escalopes can be eaten with a salad if preceded by a *primo piatto* or served with some side dishes if eaten as a one-course meal, such as Baked Tomatoes with Breadcrumbs (*see page 117*) and Chunky Olive Oil and Parmesan Mash (*see page 112*).

INGREDIENTS *1 tablespoon olive oil* ‖ *1 garlic clove, thinly sliced* ‖ *4 veal escalopes, about 125 g (4 oz) each* ‖ *seasoned plain flour, for coating* ‖ *150 ml (¼ pint) dry white wine* ‖ *6 basil leaves, torn* ‖ *salt and pepper (optional)*

ONE Heat the oil in a large frying pan over a low heat. Add the garlic and cook, stirring, for 1 minute. Increase the heat to high. **TWO** Pat the meat dry with kitchen paper, then coat it on both sides in the seasoned flour. Add the escalopes to the hot pan and cook for 2 minutes on each side until just golden, then remove from the pan and set aside. **THREE** Pour the wine into the pan and stir well with a wooden spoon to loosen any sediment on the base of the pan. Stir in the basil and leave to simmer gently for 1 minute. Adjust the seasoning, if necessary, then return the escalopes to the pan. Turn a couple of times in the sauce and serve immediately.

Serves 4

NUTRIENT ANALYSIS PER SERVING 809 kJ – 192 kcal – 29 g protein – 2 g carbohydrate – 0 g sugars – 5 g fat – 1 g saturates – 0 g fibre – 75 mg sodium

HEALTHY TIP Veal is a very low-fat and nutritious meat. It contains iron, though not as much as beef, and is also an excellent source of B-group vitamins such as thiamin, riboflavin, nicotinic acid and pantothenic acid.

Veal escalopes *alla pizzaiola*

You can't eat a lighter meat dish than veal escalopes. The *pizzaiola* sauce, made with tomato, oregano and capers, adds a fresh, summery taste to the dish and can also be served spooned over grilled chicken breasts or cod fillets. Serve this dish with Broccoli with Garlic and Chilli (*see page 113*) and/or Chunky Olive Oil and Parmesan Mash (*see page 112*).

INGREDIENTS *1 garlic clove, peeled but kept whole* ‖ *1 tablespoon olive oil* ‖ *4 veal escalopes, about 125 g (4 oz) each* ‖ *seasoned plain flour, for coating* ‖ *75 ml (3 fl oz) dry white wine* ‖ *½ quantity Basic Tomato Sauce* (see page 17*)* ‖ *½ teaspoon dried oregano* ‖ *2 tablespoons capers, soaked and drained* ‖ *salt and pepper (optional)*

ONE Bruise the garlic clove with a large cook's knife (*see page 9*). Heat the oil in a large frying pan over a low heat. Add the garlic and cook, turning occasionally, for 10 minutes. Remove and discard the garlic and increase the heat to high. **TWO** Pat the meat dry with kitchen paper, then coat it on both sides in seasoned flour. Add the escalopes to the hot pan and cook for 1 minute on each side until just golden, then remove them from the pan and set aside. **THREE** Pour the wine into the pan, stir well with a wooden spoon to loosen any sediment on the base of the pan and cook for 1 minute. Add the sauce, oregano and capers and bring to the boil. Adjust the seasoning, if necessary, then return the escalopes to the pan. Turn a couple of times in the sauce and serve immediately.

Serves 4

NUTRIENT ANALYSIS PER SERVING 890 kJ – 211 kcal – 30 g protein – 7 g carbohydrate – 5 g sugars – 6 g fat – 1 g saturates – 1 g fibre – 150 mg sodium

HEALTHY TIP Tomatoes are a good source of antioxidants, which may protect against cancer. They also contain salicylate, which may cause sensitivity in some people.

Ossobuco alla Milanese

This is a landmark of Italian cooking, but few would regard it as a light dish. Most recipes call for frying the *ossobuco* in butter, then cooking it in a rich tomato sauce. With such flavoursome meat, this is not strictly necessary, so here olive oil is used and the meat is cooked *in bianco*, meaning 'without tomatoes'. The result is lighter but equally luscious – especially once you have added a fresh scattering of *gremolata*. Serve with Chunky Olive Oil and Parmesan Mash (*see page 112*) – a healthier accompaniment than the traditional buttery saffron risotto.

INGREDIENTS *1 tablespoon olive oil* ‖ *1 onion, finely chopped* ‖ *1 celery stick, finely chopped* ‖ *1 garlic clove, finely chopped* ‖ *4* ossobuchi *(veal shank 'steaks'), about 300–325 g (10–11 oz) each* ‖ *seasoned plain flour, for coating* ‖ *1 bay leaf* ‖ *175 ml (6 fl oz) dry white wine* ‖ *175 ml (6 fl oz) Beef Stock (see page 19) or weak shop-bought beef stock* ‖ *salt and pepper*

GREMOLATA *grated rind of ½ lemon* ‖ *1 garlic clove, finely chopped* ‖ *1 tablespoon roughly chopped flat leaf parsley*

ONE Heat half the oil in a heavy-based saucepan over a low heat. Add the onion and celery and cook, stirring occasionally, for 8 minutes. Add the garlic and cook, stirring, for a further 2 minutes until the vegetables are soft and just beginning to colour. Remove from the pan and set aside. **TWO** To prevent the meat from breaking up while cooking, tie a length of kitchen string around the girth of each *ossobuco*. Pat the meat dry with kitchen paper, then coat lightly in seasoned flour. Heat the remaining oil in the same pan over a medium heat, add the meat and cook for 5–6 minutes on each side until golden. Return the vegetables to the pan and add the bay leaf and half the wine. Simmer until the wine has evaporated, then turn the meat and add the remaining wine. Once that has evaporated, pour in the stock and bring to the boil. Cover with a tight-fitting lid and cook over a very low heat for 1 hour until the meat is very tender, adding a little water if the pan dries out. **THREE** Combine the *gremolata* ingredients and scatter over the meat, cover and cook for a further 5 minutes. Transfer the *ossobuchi* to 4 serving plates. You will need 2 tablespoons of sauce per serving, so add some boiling water to the pan if the liquid is too reduced, bring to the boil and adjust the seasoning. Spoon the sauce over the meat and serve immediately.

Serves 4

NUTRIENT ANALYSIS PER SERVING 1236 kJ – 295 kcal – 32 g protein – 6 g carbohydrate – 3 g sugars – 13 g fat – 5 g saturates – 1 g fibre – 133 mg sodium

HEALTHY TIP Celery is high in vitamin C and is also a source of potassium and folic acid.

Carpaccio

Carpaccio can be a starter or a main course – it really depends on how hungry you are. In summer, a light *antipasto* lunch can be followed by carpaccio. It is also an ideal choice if you fancy a light meat course after a *primo piatto*. The meat can be dressed with a variety of different toppings, like a light homemade mayonnaise, or a more unusual topping, such as Salsa Verde (*see page 17*), Parmesan cheese and shredded radicchio. Here, it is complemented by the unique earthy flavour of black truffle.

INGREDIENTS *450 g (14½ oz) beef fillet, trimmed ‖ 50 g (2 oz) wild rocket ‖ 1–2 teaspoons extra virgin olive oil ‖ black truffle, for shaving, or 1 teaspoon truffle oil ‖ 40 g (1½ oz) fresh Parmesan cheese shavings ‖ salt and pepper*

ONE Wrap the beef in clingfilm and place in the freezer for 30–40 minutes before planning to serve, to firm up and make it easier to slice thinly. **TWO** Unwrap the beef and, using a mandoline or long, sharp knife, slice it as thinly as possible. Arrange the slices on 4 plates in a single layer, slightly overlapping. **THREE** If using truffle shavings, toss the rocket in 2 teaspoons of extra virgin olive oil and season with salt and pepper. Arrange it evenly over the meat, then serve with a scattering of truffle and Parmesan shavings. If using truffle oil, dress the rocket with 1 teaspoon each of olive oil and truffle oil, season with salt and pepper and serve with Parmesan shavings.

Serves 4

NUTRIENT ANALYSIS PER SERVING 906 kJ – 217 kcal – 28 g protein – 0 g carbohydrate – 0 g sugars – 12 g fat – 5 g saturates – 1 g fibre – 176 mg sodium

HEALTHY TIP Beef is a fairly low-fat meat, but you should make sure you trim off any visible fat before slicing. Beef is also a very good source of iron and B vitamins.

Meatballs with bay leaves and white wine

Much lighter than meatballs in tomato sauce, this dish is a great choice for a weekday family meal. The meatballs are delicious served with the Peperonata (*see page 123*) in summer, or on a cold day, try it with the Chunky Olive Oil and Parmesan Mash (*see page 112*).

INGREDIENTS *2 teaspoons olive oil* ‖ *150 ml (¼ pint) dry white wine* ‖ *3 bay leaves* ‖ *grated rind of 1 lemon* ‖ *salt and pepper*

MEATBALLS *1 slice of white bread, crust removed* ‖ *5 tablespoons semi-skimmed milk* ‖ *450 g (14½ oz) lean minced veal (or beef if veal is not available)* ‖ *½ small onion, finely chopped* ‖ *1 garlic clove, crushed* ‖ *1 tablespoon roughly chopped flat leaf parsley* ‖ *1 egg white* ‖ *1 tablespoon freshly grated Parmesan cheese* ‖ *salt and pepper*

ONE To make the meatballs, break the bread into 1 cm (½ inch) pieces and soak in the milk until all the milk has been absorbed and the bread starts to fall apart. **TWO** Place the meat in a large bowl and break it up with a fork. Add the soaked bread and the remaining meatball ingredients, then season lightly with salt and pepper. Work the mixture together with your hands until the ingredients are well combined, then shape into 12 meatballs. **THREE** Heat the oil in a large frying pan in which the meatballs will fit comfortably in a single layer. Add the meatballs and cook over a medium to high heat, turning frequently, for 10–12 minutes until golden brown all over. Add the wine, bay leaves and lemon rind and simmer gently, turning the meatballs occasionally, for a further 10 minutes until cooked through. Serve immediately.

Serves 4

NUTRIENT ANALYSIS PER SERVING 1040 kJ – 248 kcal – 26 g protein – 6 g carbohydrate – 2 g sugars – 11 g fat – 4 g saturates – 1 g fibre – 194 mg sodium

HEALTHY TIP When wine is used in cooking a proportion of the alcohol will be lost in the cooking process. Alcohol is quite a concentrated source of energy, providing 7 kcal (29 kJ) per gram, so brisk boiling of wine in the cooking process will reduce the calorie content (and the alcoholic effect) of the dish.

T-bone *alla Fiorentina*

The Florentines are so proud of this dish that in 1991 they even founded the Accademia della Fiorentina, a body that has laid down the regulations for what constitutes a real *Fiorentina* steak. The rules are strict, specifying the Tuscan meat to be used, the minimum and maximum weight and thickness of the steak and how the steaks need to be cooked over oak embers. This recipe uses the smallest weight specified and, for reasons of practicality, the suggested method of cooking is on a barbecue or in a griddle pan. Ask your butcher for top-quality beef, preferably from a young animal. Traditionally, the meat is served without a sauce, perhaps with some green vegetables on the side. If you really need a sauce, serve it with some Salsa Verde (*see page 17*) or Pesto (*see page 44*). The Accademia wouldn't approve, but they go together beautifully!

INGREDIENTS *1 T-bone steak, about 625 g (1¼ lb) and 2.5 cm (1 inch) thick* ‖ *2 teaspoons olive oil* ‖ *salt and pepper*

ONE Heat a ridged cast-iron griddle pan over a high heat until it is searing hot, or if barbecuing, get the coals to the stage where there are no more flames and the coals are covered with a thin layer of grey ash. **TWO** Without flavouring or seasoning it in any way, place the steak in the griddle pan or on the barbecue and cook for 4–5 minutes on each side until golden brown. Remove from the heat and season with salt and pepper. **THREE** Drizzle a serving platter with the oil, sit the steak on it and serve immediately.

Serves 4

NUTRIENT ANALYSIS PER SERVING 1623 kJ – 386 kcal – 63 g protein – 0 g carbohydrate – 0 g sugars – 15 g fat – 5 g saturates – 0 g fibre – 173 mg sodium

HEALTHY TIP Red meat, such as beef, has been blamed for many of the health problems that are associated with Western diets. However, when eaten in moderation, beef is a nutritious and fairly low-fat meat. It is also an excellent source of dietary iron.

Beef strips with radicchio

This Roman recipe known as *straccetti*, or 'little rags', takes minutes to prepare, making it an ideal after-work supper – with the added bonus that if you are also serving an *antipasto* or *primo piatto*, the *straccetti* won't even need a side dish. You can vary this dish by replacing the bitter-flavoured radicchio with peppery rocket.

INGREDIENTS *3 sirloin steaks, about 300 g (10 oz) each* ‖ *½ tablespoon olive oil* ‖ *2 garlic cloves, finely chopped* ‖ *150 g (5 oz) radicchio, sliced into 2.5 cm (1 inch) strips* ‖ *salt*

ONE Trim the fat from the steaks and slice the meat into very thin strips. Set aside. **TWO** Heat the oil in a heavy-based frying pan over a high heat. Add the garlic and steak strips, season with salt and stir-fry for 2 minutes until the steak is golden brown. **THREE** Add the radicchio and stir-fry until the leaves are just beginning to wilt. Serve immediately.

Serves 4

NUTRIENT ANALYSIS PER SERVING 1346 kJ – 320 kcal – 53 g protein – 1 g carbohydrate – 1 g sugars – 12 g fat – 5 g saturates – 1 g fibre – 158 mg sodium

HEALTHY TIP Radicchio is used for its colour, texture and slightly astringent taste, but like all red vegetables it is also a good source of carotene, which has antioxidant properties, and folic acid, which is important for the growth and maintenance of cells.

Roast rabbit with rosemary and white wine

Rabbit is an incredibly lean, tasty meat that can be cooked in much the same way as chicken. Sage or thyme suit its light, gamey flavour, but try experimenting with other herbs of your choice. This healthy winter warmer is delicious served with soft polenta, Braised Fennel with Wine and Black Olives (*see page 114*) or Braised Black Cabbage with Chilli and Fennel Seeds (*see page 118*).

INGREDIENTS *1 tablespoon olive oil ‖ 4 garlic cloves, unpeeled ‖ 4 sprigs of rosemary ‖ 1 bay leaf ‖ 1 rabbit, about 1.75 kg (3½ lb), cut into 8 pieces (ask your butcher to do this) ‖ 150 ml (¼ pint) dry white wine ‖ salt and pepper*

ONE Heat half the oil in a large flameproof casserole pan or roasting tin over a low heat. Add the garlic, rosemary and bay leaf and cook gently, stirring occasionally, for 5 minutes, to infuse the oil, then increase the heat to high. **TWO** Season the rabbit lightly with salt and pepper, add to the pan and cook, turning occasionally, for 10–12 minutes until golden on all sides. Pour in half the wine and bring to the boil. **THREE** Transfer the pan or tin to a preheated oven, 180°C (350°F), Gas Mark 4, and roast for 15 minutes. Remove from the oven, stir in the remaining wine and turn the rabbit pieces in the sauce. Return to the oven for a further 15 minutes before serving.

Serves 4

NUTRIENT ANALYSIS PER SERVING 1440 kJ – 343 kcal – 47 g protein – 1 g carbohydrate – 0 g sugars – 15 g fat – 5 g saturates – 0 g fibre – 144 mg sodium

HEALTHY TIP Rabbit has a low fat content, similar to that of chicken, and in the past it was used as a cheap substitute for chicken. Today we enjoy rabbit in its own right as a tasty and nutritious low-fat meat which provides a range of useful vitamins and minerals.

Grilled pork steaks with sage

Pork and sage is a favourite combination in Italy. This recipe uses a beautifully lean cut, stuffed with the perfect herb to guarantee that the steaks are flavoursome all the way through. Serve with Braised Fennel with Wine and Black Olives (*see page 114*) or Braised Black Cabbage with Chilli and Fennel Seeds (*see page 118*).

INGREDIENTS *4 pork loin steaks, about 200 g (7 oz) each* ‖ *2 garlic cloves, finely chopped* ‖ *1½ tablespoons finely chopped sage* ‖ *1 teaspoon olive oil* ‖ *salt and pepper*

ONE Cut a horizontal pocket through the centre of each pork steak. **TWO** Combine the garlic, sage and oil and rub this mixture all over the outside and inside of the pork steaks. Place in a dish, cover and leave to marinate in the refrigerator for at least 30 minutes or overnight. **THREE** Season the outside and inside of the pork steaks with salt and pepper, then place on a baking sheet lined with foil. Cook under a preheated very hot grill, about 10 cm (4 inches) from the heat, for 5 minutes. Turn the pork steaks over and cook for a further 5 minutes or until cooked through and golden.

Serves 4

NUTRIENT ANALYSIS PER SERVING 1280 kJ – 306 kcal – 42 g protein – 1 g carbohydrate – 0 g sugars – 15 g fat – 5 g saturates – 0 g fibre – 74 mg sodium

HEALTHY TIP Pork used to be a very fatty meat, but today pigs are bred to be much leaner. There is still a certain amount of invisible fat incorporated in the lean meat, which helps give pork its texture and flavour, so trim any visible fat off to keep the meat as lean as possible.

Bollito misto with salsa verde

This dish from Piedmont is a national treasure that is usually made with up to seven meats. In this version, the meat content is cut down to three lean varieties. The result is a moist, flavoursome meat feast that is light and healthy. This is a one-pot meal, with no starter or accompaniments necessary other than the Salsa Verde. Don't waste the beautiful stock. Reduce it to concentrate the flavours, then once cooled, freeze it in small containers.

INGREDIENTS *1 large onion, quartered* ‖ *2 bay leaves* ‖ *6 parsley stalks* ‖ *2 celery sticks, halved lengthways* ‖ *4 carrots* ‖ *1 ox tongue, about 1.5 kg (3 lb)* ‖ *1 boned veal shoulder joint, about 1.75 kg (3½ lb)* ‖ *1 chicken, about 1.75 kg (3½ lb)* ‖ *8 baby turnips* ‖ *8 baby onions* ‖ *Salsa Verde* (see page 17), *to serve*

ONE Place the onion, bay leaves, parsley stalks, celery and 1 carrot in a large stock pot. Fill with water and bring to the boil. Add the ox tongue and return to the boil. Skim off any scum that rises to the surface and reduce the heat to a gentle simmer. Cover and cook for 1 hour, skimming occasionally. **TWO** Add the veal and simmer gently for 30 minutes, then add the chicken and more boiling water if necessary. Bring to the boil, skim, then reduce the heat and simmer gently for 1 hour. **THREE** Remove and discard the carrot and celery. Quarter the remaining carrots lengthways and add to the pan with the turnips and baby onions. Simmer gently for a further 30 minutes. **FOUR** Remove the meats from the pan and leave to rest for 5 minutes. Add a ladleful of cold water to the pan and bring to the boil again, to encourage any fat and scum to rise to the surface. Skim and repeat. **FIVE** Meanwhile, skin the tongue and cut it into 5 mm (¼ inch) slices. Slice the other meats to the same thickness and arrange in the centre of a large serving platter, keeping separate. Spoon over some of the stock and drain the stock pot, reserving the stock to use in other recipes (see above). Arrange the vegetables around the meats and serve immediately with the Salsa Verde.

Serves 8–10

NUTRIENT ANALYSIS PER SERVING 2947 kJ – 706 kcal – 88 g protein – 9 g carbohydrate – 8 g sugars – 36 g fat – 5 g saturates – 3 g fibre – 900 mg sodium

HEALTHY TIP Tongue has a higher fat content than chicken and, unlike chicken, the fat in tongue is not mainly in the skin. To reduce the fat content of the dish skim off as much fat as possible from the stock.

Contorni –
vegetables and pulses

Braised artichokes with mint

This Roman dish is possibly one of the most delicate yet delicious recipes for artichoke. It is often prepared with medium-sized artichokes, but these tender baby ones are equally tasty and, being much simpler to prepare, are ideal if you are a novice artichoke cook. Serve as an accompaniment to meat or poultry, or as an *antipasto*.

INGREDIENTS *12 baby artichokes* ‖ *juice of ½ lemon* ‖ *2 tablespoons finely chopped parsley* ‖ *2 tablespoons finely chopped mint* ‖ *2 garlic cloves, crushed* ‖ *2 tablespoons olive oil* ‖ *salt and pepper*

ONE To prepare the artichokes, pull off the tough outer leaves, exposing the paler tender leaves, then cut about 2.5 cm (1 inch) off the top. Trim the stalks, leaving about 3.5 cm (1½ inches), then peel with a potato peeler to reveal the lighter core. Baby artichokes have an edible tender choke, but if you are using larger ones, open the central leaves and scoop out and discard the hairy choke with a teaspoon. As you prepare them, place the artichokes in a bowl of cold water with the lemon juice, to prevent discoloration. **TWO** Combine the parsley, mint and garlic and season with salt. Drain the artichokes and place a large pinch of the herb mixture in the central cavity of each one. Stand the artichokes, stuffed side down, in a heavy-based saucepan in which they fit snugly in a single layer. Pour in enough water to come a quarter of the way up the artichokes, then drizzle with the oil and scatter with the remaining herb mixture. Season with salt and pepper. **THREE** Bring to the boil over a high heat, then reduce the heat to a gentle simmer. Cover with greaseproof paper, to help retain a steamy atmosphere close to the artichokes, and a tight-fitting lid. Cook for 20–25 minutes or until tender when pierced with a fork. Leave the artichokes to cool before serving. They are best eaten just warm or at room temperature.

Serves 4

NUTRIENT ANALYSIS PER SERVING 453 kJ – 109 kcal – 4 g protein – 10 g carbohydrate – 0 g sugars – 6 g fat – 1 g saturates – 1 g fibre – 52 mg sodium

HEALTHY TIP Artichokes contain the compounds cynarin and sylmarin, both of which are thought to help the liver regenerate healthy tissue. Artichokes are also a good source of several minerals, including phosphorus, magnesium, manganese and chromium.

Chunky olive oil and Parmesan mash

Dishes with a rich sauce such as the *Ossobuco alla Milanese* (*see page 96*) or Roast Rabbit with Rosemary and White Wine (*see page 104*) call for an accompaniment to soak up their tasty juices. This light mash is perfect for the job. Flavoured with freshly stirred-through extra virgin olive oil and Parmesan cheese, it has no need for heavy-duty saturated fats such as cream or butter.

INGREDIENTS *875 g (1¾ lb) waxy potatoes, peeled* ‖ *2 tablespoons freshly grated Parmesan cheese* ‖ *3 tablespoons olive oil* ‖ *salt and pepper*

ONE Place the potatoes in a saucepan and pour in enough water to cover. **TWO** Bring to the boil over a high heat, then reduce the heat and simmer for 20–25 minutes until tender. **THREE** Drain, return the potatoes to the pan and roughly mash, leaving large chunks of potato. **FOUR** Season with salt and pepper, stir in the Parmesan and oil and serve.

Serves 4 as a side dish

NUTRIENT ANALYSIS PER SERVING 1095 kJ – 260 kcal – 7 g protein – 38 g carbohydrate – 1 g sugars – 10 g fat – 2 g saturates – 4 g fibre – 70 mg sodium

HEALTHY TIP Potatoes are a good source of vitamin C, partly because we tend to eat them in larger amounts and more often than other vegetables. Peel potatoes as thinly as possible because most of the vitamin C content is close to the skin. Try to cook them as soon as possible after peeling.

Broccoli with garlic and chilli

You can use regular or sprouting broccoli for this dish. This combination also makes a delicious pasta sauce if you increase the quantity of oil to 3 tablespoons and cook the broccoli florets until they are so soft that they start to fall apart.

INGREDIENTS *625 g (1¼ lb) broccoli* ‖ *1 tablespoon olive oil* ‖ *2 garlic cloves, finely sliced* ‖ *1 mild red chilli, finely sliced into rounds* ‖ *salt*

ONE Cut the broccoli into small florets and cook in a large saucepan of salted boiling water for 3–4 minutes until just tender. Drain well. **TWO** Heat the oil in a large frying pan over a low heat. Add the garlic and chilli and cook, stirring, for 2 minutes, being careful that the garlic doesn't colour. Increase the heat to high, add the broccoli and stir-fry in the oil for 1 minute until beginning to char. Serve immediately.

Serves 4 as a side dish

NUTRIENT ANALYSIS PER SERVING 327 kJ – 79 kcal – 7 g protein – 3 g carbohydrate – 2 g sugars – 4 g fat – 1 g saturates – 2 g fibre – 13 mg sodium

HEALTHY TIP Broccoli is a very good source of folic acid, which is important for cell growth and maintenance, particularly in early pregnancy. Folic acid is destroyed by heat, so it is advisable to cook broccoli for as short a time as possible.

Braised fennel with wine and black olives

In terms of ingredients, this dish is similar to the Fennel, Orange and Olive Salad (*see page* 35), but the result couldn't be more different. Fennel undergoes a complete transformation when cooked, from a fresh, crisp texture and aromatic aniseed flavour to a robust-tasting vegetable that is tender yet with a juicy bite. Serve with a simple fish or meat dish. It would complement the Grilled Red Mullet with Thyme and Lemon (*see page* 76), Roast Chicken with Rosemary (*see page* 92) or the Grilled Pork Steaks with Sage (*see page* 106).

INGREDIENTS *2 large fennel bulbs* ‖ *1 tablespoon olive oil* ‖ *2 garlic cloves, unpeeled* ‖ *large pinch of crushed dried red chillies* ‖ *2 teaspoons roughly chopped rosemary leaves* ‖ *125 ml (4 fl oz) dry white wine* ‖ *40 g (1½ oz) pitted black olives, roughly chopped* ‖ *juice of 1 small orange* ‖ *salt (optional)*

ONE Cut the fennel bulbs in half, then cut each half into 4 wedges. Place in a large, heavy-based frying pan and stir in the oil, garlic, chillies and rosemary. Cook over a medium heat, stirring occasionally, for 10 minutes until lightly golden. **TWO** Pour in the wine and bring to the boil over a high heat. Add the olives, reduce the heat and simmer, uncovered, stirring occasionally, for 15–20 minutes, until tender. **THREE** Increase the heat and reduce any remaining sauce until the fennel begins to caramelize. Pour in the orange juice and cook, stirring, until that too has reduced. Taste, adding salt if necessary, then serve.

Serves 4 as a side dish

NUTRIENT ANALYSIS PER SERVING 350 kJ – 85 kcal – 2 g protein – 5 g carbohydrate – 4 g sugars – 4 g fat – 1 g saturates – 1 g fibre – 246 mg sodium

HEALTHY TIP Although folic acid tends to be found in green vegetables, fennel bulbs do provide a significant amount, and are also a good source of fibre and minerals. Folic acid is heat sensitive, so the longer the cooking process the more will be lost.

Baked aubergine with tomato sauce and mozzarella

Melanzane alla Parmigiana is one of those classic dishes that you will find on Italian menus throughout the world. The grilled aubergines in this version make it much lighter than the original, where the aubergines are fried in copious amounts of olive oil. Serve on its own, as an alternative to pasta, or as a side dish to the Meatballs with Bay Leaves and White Wine (*see page 100*).

INGREDIENTS *250 ml (8 fl oz) passata* ‖ *5 large basil leaves, torn* ‖ *1 garlic clove, crushed* ‖ *1 kg (2 lb) aubergines* ‖ *250 g (8 oz) mozzarella cheese (drained weight), roughly chopped* ‖ *4 tablespoons freshly grated Parmesan cheese* ‖ *salt*

ONE Combine the passata, basil and garlic in a bowl. Season with salt, cover and leave to marinate while you grill the aubergines. **TWO** Cut the aubergines lengthways into slices about 5 mm (¼ inch) thick. Heat a ridged cast-iron griddle pan over a high heat until it is searing hot, add the aubergine slices and cook for 2 minutes on each side until charred on the outside and soft all the way to the centre. If the outside is colouring too quickly, reduce the temperature to give the centre a chance to cook. Set aside. **THREE** Assemble the ingredients in an oven dish or roasting tin 25 x 17 cm (10 x 6¾ inches). Spread the base with a couple of tablespoons of the tomato sauce, then top with a single layer of aubergine slices so that they slightly overlap. Season lightly with salt, then top with a third of the remaining tomato sauce. Scatter with one-third of the mozzarella and 1 tablespoon of Parmesan. Repeat the layers, starting with the aubergine slices, until all the ingredients are used up, finishing with 2 tablespoons of Parmesan. **FOUR** Bake in a preheated oven, 180°C (350°F), Gas Mark 4, for 30 minutes. Leave to cool for 5 minutes before serving.

Serves 6 as a side dish or 4 as a main course

NUTRIENT ANALYSIS PER SERVING 727 kJ – 174 kcal – 14 g protein – 5 g carbohydrate – 4 g sugars – 11 g fat – 7 g saturates – 4 g fibre – 328 mg sodium

HEALTHY TIP Mozzarella cheese is a very good source of calcium, and is low in fat compared to other cheeses. Parmesan has a high fat content, so try not to use more than the recipe suggests.

Baked tomatoes with breadcrumbs

Gently cooking whole or halved tomatoes over a long period concentrates their flavour without them losing their shape. You can serve these with any fish or meat main course that doesn't already have tomatoes in it. They are particularly delicious with the Monkfish Skewers Wrapped in Prosciutto (*see page 78*).

INGREDIENTS *4 ripe tomatoes, halved* ‖ *2 teaspoons olive oil* ‖ *1½ tablespoons roughly chopped mint* ‖ *2 garlic cloves, finely chopped* ‖ *3 tablespoons dried breadcrumbs* ‖ *1 tablespoon finely chopped capers* ‖ *salt*

ONE Line a roasting tin in which the tomatoes will fit snugly in a single layer with greaseproof paper. Arrange the tomatoes in the tin, cut side up, and drizzle with half the oil. Season lightly with salt and bake in a preheated oven, 150°C (300°F), Gas Mark 2, for 1 hour. **TWO** Increase the oven temperature to 220°C (425°F), Gas Mark 7. Remove the tin from the oven. Combine the remaining ingredients, then scatter over the roasted tomatoes. Return to the oven and roast for a further 8–10 minutes until golden and crisp. Serve warm as a side dish or at room temperature as an *antipasto*.

Serves 4 as a side dish or 4–6 as part of an antipasto *selection*

NUTRIENT ANALYSIS PER SERVING 265 kJ – 63 kcal – 2 g protein – 9 g carbohydrate – 5 g sugars – 2 g fat – 0 g saturates – 2 g fibre – 85 mg sodium

HEALTHY TIP Tomatoes are a great source of vitamin C, and are also valued for their betacarotene content which gives them valuable antioxidant properties. Vitamin C, in common with the other water-soluble vitamins (the B group) is heat sensitive, so some of the vitamin will be lost in the cooking process.

Braised black cabbage with chilli and fennel seeds

This recipe uses the classic Italian technique for cooking leafy vegetables. First you blanch the vegetable in boiling water until tender, then, once drained, it is sautéed in a frying pan with garlic, olive oil and any other flavourings you choose. You can prepare spinach and Swiss chard in exactly the same way, replacing the fennel seeds with a squeeze of lemon juice. Serve this cabbage dish with Roast Rabbit with Rosemary and White Wine (*see page 104*) or the Grilled Pork Steaks with Sage (*see page 106*).

INGREDIENTS *1.5 kg (3 lb) black cabbage* ‖ *1 tablespoon olive oil* ‖ *2 garlic cloves, thinly sliced* ‖ *1 teaspoon fennel seeds* ‖ *½ dried red chilli, chopped* ‖ *extra virgin olive oil, for drizzling (optional)* ‖ *salt*

ONE Remove the thick stalks from the cabbage by holding the stems with one hand and using the other hand to strip away the leaves. Cook in a saucepan of boiling water for 6–7 minutes until just tender, then drain thoroughly. **TWO** Heat the oil in a large frying pan over a low heat. Add the garlic, fennel seeds and chilli and cook, stirring, for 3 minutes. Stir in the cabbage, season with salt and cook, stirring, for 3–4 minutes until the cabbage has completely wilted and absorbed the flavours. Drizzle with extra virgin olive oil just before serving, if you like.

Serves 4 as a side dish

NUTRIENT ANALYSIS PER SERVING 463 kJ – 110 kcal – 5 g protein – 15 g carbohydrate – 12 g sugars – 4 g fat – 0 g saturates – 12 g fibre – 30 mg sodium

HEALTHY TIP Red and black cabbage are an excellent source of folic acid and also provide carotene, the precursor of vitamin A. With the addition of the fennel seeds this dish is a good source of fibre.

Grilled radicchio with Parmesan

Radicchio is a bitter leaf that grows either in a round shape, similar to that of iceberg lettuce, or in a pointed, loose form that resembles chicory. The latter is called radicchio di Treviso and works particularly well in this recipe, with some of the grated Parmesan falling between the looser leaves. The bitterness of radicchio makes it the perfect accompaniment to meat or poultry. Try it with the T-bone *alla Fiorentina* (*see page 101*) or the Veal Escalopes with Basil (*see page 93*).

INGREDIENTS *4 radicchio di Treviso or 2 round radicchio* ‖ *1½ tablespoons olive oil* ‖ *4 tablespoons freshly grated Parmesan cheese* ‖ *salt and pepper*

ONE If using radicchio di Treviso, cut in half lengthways. Cut the round radicchio into quarters. **TWO** Brush all sides of the radicchio with the oil, then season with salt and pepper. Place on a baking sheet and cook under a preheated medium grill, about 12 cm (5 inches) from the heat, for 10 minutes. The leaves will darken in colour but they should not be allowed to char, so reduce the heat or increase the distance between the radicchio and the heat if necessary. **THREE** Scatter the Parmesan over the grilled radicchio, then return to the grill for 30 seconds until the cheese has melted. Serve immediately, or leave to cool to room temperature if serving as an *antipasto*.

Serves 4 as a side dish or 4–6 as part of an antipasto *selection*

NUTRIENT ANALYSIS PER SERVING 386 kJ – 93 kcal – 4 g protein – 3 g carbohydrate – 1 g sugars – 8 g fat – 3 g saturates – 2 g fibre – 110 mg sodium

HEALTHY TIP Radicchio's red colouring means it is a source of carotene and has useful antioxidant properties. Radicchio also contains folic acid.

Green beans with lemon and garlic

This refreshing side dish makes a simple accompaniment to a light meal. Serve with fish or meat dishes, such as Roast Rabbit with Rosemary and White Wine (*see page 104*) or Stuffed Tuna Rolls with White Wine (*see page 84*).

INGREDIENTS *300 g (10 oz) green beans* ‖ *½ tablespoon extra virgin olive oil* ‖ *grated rind of 1 lemon* ‖ *1 garlic clove, crushed* ‖ *1 tablespoon roughly chopped flat leaf parsley* ‖ *salt*

ONE Cook the beans in a saucepan of salted boiling water for 3–4 minutes until just tender but still with a bite. Drain thoroughly and transfer to a bowl. **TWO** Add the remaining ingredients and season with salt. Toss to combine and serve.

Serves 4 as a side dish

NUTRIENT ANALYSIS PER SERVING 136 kJ – 33 kcal – 2 g protein – 3 g carbohydrate – 2 g sugars – 2 g fat – 0 g saturates – 3 g fibre – 30 mg sodium

HEALTHY TIP Green beans provide a range of vitamins including vitamin C, folic acid and carotene as well as some minerals and trace elements. Steaming, rather than boiling, will preserve the vitamin content better.

Peperonata

This southern Italian dish of stewed peppers in tomato sauce is a firm family favourite throughout Italy. Perhaps it is because it can be served in so many different guises. As well as a side dish, it is delicious spooned over soft polenta, stirred into pasta or even eaten cold as an *antipasto*.

INGREDIENTS *2 large red peppers, grilled, skinned, cored and deseeded (see page 22)* ‖ *2 large yellow peppers, grilled, skinned, cored and deseeded (see page 22)* ‖ *2 teaspoons olive oil* ‖ *1 small onion, finely chopped* ‖ *2 garlic cloves, finely chopped* ‖ *400 g (13 oz) can plum tomatoes, roughly chopped* ‖ *6 large basil leaves, torn* ‖ *extra virgin olive oil, for drizzling (optional)* ‖ *salt*

ONE Cut the peppers into wide strips and set aside. **TWO** Heat the olive oil in a heavy-based saucepan over a low heat. Add the onion and cook, stirring occasionally, for 10 minutes until softened. Add the garlic and cook, stirring, for 1 minute. Add the tomatoes and their juice and pepper strips. Season with salt and bring to the boil. Reduce the heat to a gentle simmer and cook, stirring occasionally, for 25 minutes. **THREE** Stir the basil into the pan and cook for a further 5–10 minutes until the sauce has reduced. Drizzle with extra virgin olive oil before serving, if you like.

Serves 4 as a side dish

NUTRIENT ANALYSIS PER SERVING 303 kJ – 72 kcal – 3 g protein – 12 g carbohydrate – 10 g sugars – 2 g fat – 0 g saturates – 3 g fibre – 44 mg sodium

HEALTHY TIP Red and yellow peppers are a particularly good source of betacarotene and therefore have excellent antioxidant properties. Antioxidants are thought to prevent cancers by removing the possibly carcinogenic free radicals occuring naturally and as a result of cooking processes in some foods.

Cannellini beans with sage and tomato

This warming and wholesome side dish is kept fresh and light with the addition of barely cooked tomatoes. It is particularly good when served as an accompaniment to meat dishes.

INGREDIENTS *250 g (8 oz) fresh shelled cannellini beans or 200 g (7 oz) dried cannellini beans, soaked in cold water overnight, drained and rinsed, or 2 x 400 g (13 oz) cans cannellini beans, drained and rinsed ‖ 1 bay leaf (optional) ‖ 2 garlic cloves, unpeeled (optional) ‖ 2 teaspoons olive oil ‖ 1 red onion, finely sliced ‖ 5 sage leaves, roughly chopped ‖ pinch of crushed dried red chillies ‖ 2 tomatoes, skinned (see page 9) and chopped ‖ extra virgin olive oil, for drizzling (optional) ‖ salt*

ONE If using fresh beans, place in a saucepan, add enough cold water to cover by about 5 cm (2 inches) and add the bay leaf, and the garlic if you like. Bring to the boil and skim off any scum that rises to the surface. Reduce the heat to a simmer and cook, uncovered, for 25–30 minutes or until tender, then drain, reserving the garlic cloves, if using. If using presoaked dried beans, cook as for the fresh beans, but they will take about 1½ hours to become tender. The canned beans are ready to use. **TWO** Heat the olive oil in a large, heavy-based frying pan over a low heat. Add the onion, sage and chillies and cook, stirring occasionally, for 10 minutes until the onion is softened. Remove the garlic cloves from the cooked beans and squeeze the flesh out of the skin into the frying pan. If using canned beans simply add 1 chopped garlic clove to the frying pan at this stage. Cook, stirring, for 1 minute, then add the beans and the tomatoes. Season with salt and cook, stirring, for 3–5 minutes before serving, drizzled with a little extra virgin olive oil, if you like.

Serves 4 as a side dish

NUTRIENT ANALYSIS PER SERVING 727 kJ – 170 kcal – 11 g protein – 30 g carbohydrate – 4 g sugars – 2 g fat – 0 g saturates – 4 g fibre – 7 mg sodium

HEALTHY TIP Beans are a particularly useful food for vegetarians, providing a good source of protein, carbohydrate, iron and other minerals and trace elements. They are also a good source of fibre.

Fresh peas with prosciutto

The sweet refreshing flavours of peas and mint are delicious when paired with a salty cured meat such as *prosciutto crudo* or speck. Serve with Roast Chicken with Rosemary (*see page 92*), Veal Escalopes with Basil (*see page 93*) or Stuffed Squid with Herbs and Anchovies (*see page 73*).

INGREDIENTS *1 tablespoon olive oil* ‖ *1 small onion, finely chopped* ‖ *125 g (4 oz) thickly sliced prosciutto crudo, cut into strips* ‖ *400 g (13 oz) shelled fresh peas or frozen peas, defrosted* ‖ *1 tablespoon roughly chopped mint* ‖ *4 tablespoons dry white wine* ‖ *salt (optional)*

ONE Heat the oil in a frying pan over a medium heat. Add the onion and cook, stirring occasionally, for 5 minutes. Stir in the prosciutto strips and cook, stirring, for 2–3 minutes until crisp. **TWO** Stir in the peas, mint and wine and cook for 5 minutes if using fresh peas, or 2 minutes if using defrosted frozen peas. Season with salt, if necessary, and serve immediately.

Serves 4 as a side dish

NUTRIENT ANALYSIS PER SERVING 804 kJ – 194 kcal – 16 g protein – 13 g carbohydrate – 3 g sugars – 8 g fat – 2 g saturates – 5 g fibre – 627 mg sodium

HEALTHY TIP Frozen peas often have a higher vitamin content than fresh peas, because they are frozen so soon after picking. Fresh peas bought from a greengrocer may have been picked some time previously and will have lost a proportion of their vitamin content in storage. Small peas, for example 'petit pois', have a higher fibre content than larger ones.

Pane e pizze –
breads and pizzas

Rustic loaf

No Italian meal is complete without some bread at the table. A chunky white loaf is always at hand for making sandwiches and bruschette, as well as, most deliciously, to mop up any juices from your dish! The use of *semola di grano duro* in this recipe adds weight and a real rustic quality to the loaf.

INGREDIENTS *15 g (½ oz) fresh yeast or 2 teaspoons dried yeast* ‖ *large pinch of caster sugar* ‖ *300 ml (½ pint) lukewarm water* ‖ *375 g (12 oz) Italian 00 flour or plain flour, plus extra for dusting* ‖ *1½ teaspoons salt* ‖ *125 g (4 oz)* **semola di grano duro** ‖ *1 tablespoon olive oil, plus extra for oiling*

ONE Dissolve the yeast in a bowl with the sugar, measurement water and half the 00 or plain flour. Cover with a moist cloth and leave to stand in a warm place for 15 minutes. **TWO** Stir the salt into the remaining flours, then tip the flour mixture into the now-foamy paste. Add the oil and stir the mixture with one hand until all the ingredients have combined to form a moist dough. Knead the dough on a floured work surface for about 10 minutes until smooth and elastic. Place the dough in an oiled bowl, cover with a moist cloth and leave to rise in a warm place for 1½ hours until doubled in size. **THREE** Knead the risen dough on a floured work surface for 1 minute, then shape into a large ball. Transfer to a lightly floured baking sheet and cover with a moist cloth. Leave to rise in a warm place for 1 hour, until it feels light and pillowy to the touch. **FOUR** When the dough is ready, place a roasting tin filled with water at the bottom of a preheated oven, 220°C (425°F), Gas Mark 7, which will create steam and help give the bread a good crust. Using a sharp knife, cut 4 slashes across the top of the loaf and dust lightly with 00 or plain flour. Bake for 35–40 minutes or until the base sounds hollow when tapped. Leave to cool on a wire rack. The loaf is best eaten on the day it is baked.

Makes 1 large loaf

NUTRIENT ANALYSIS PER SLICE (1 LOAF = 12 SLICES) 654 kJ – 154 kcal – 5 g protein – 32 g carbohydrate – 1 g sugars – 2 g fat – 0 g saturates – 2 g fibre – 2 mg sodium

HEALTHY TIP Bread is a very good source of slow release carbohydrate, an excellent long-lasting energy source. It also contains a moderate amount of protein. The protein in bread and flour becomes of greater value if it is mixed with other protein sources to complement it, for example, in a sandwich.

Grissini

These are the crisp breadsticks you see in Italian restaurants. The idea is that you pick at them while you wait for your food to arrive. Alternatively, wrap some Parma ham around them and serve them as an *antipasto*. You can vary the topping by replacing the sesame seeds with a scattering of fennel seeds and grated Parmesan.

INGREDIENTS *½ quantity Basic Pizza Dough (see page 15)* ‖ *plain flour, for dusting* ‖ *olive oil, for glazing* ‖ *2 tablespoons sesame seeds*

ONE Make the pizza dough following the method on page 15, but in Step 2, shape the dough into a single ball, rather than 4, before leaving to rise for 1 hour. **TWO** Roll the dough out on a lightly floured work surface into a rectangle about 1 cm (½ inch) thick. Cut the dough into 1 cm (½ inch) strips along the length of the rectangle, then place the strips on a lightly floured baking sheet. **THREE** Brush the dough strips lightly with oil to glaze, then scatter with the sesame seeds. Bake in a preheated oven, 200°C (400°F), Gas Mark 6, for 6–8 minutes until golden. Transfer the breadsticks to a wire rack to cool and crisp up. The grissini will keep well in an airtight container for about 1 week.

Makes about 40 grissini

NUTRIENT ANALYSIS PER GRISSINI 116 kJ – 27 kcal – 1 g protein – 5 g carbohydrate – 0 g sugars – 1 g fat – 0 g saturates – 0 g fibre – 25 mg sodium

HEALTHY TIP Sesame seeds are a good source of calcium, and make a tasty addition when sprinkled on some vegetables.

Sun-dried tomato ciabatta

To make the perfect ciabatta, with a light airy texture, you need a starter dough. Leave it to rise for one day, then you can complete the dough the next day.

INGREDIENTS

DAY 1 *5 g (¼ oz) fresh yeast or ¼ teaspoon dried yeast* ‖ *pinch of caster sugar* ‖ *150 ml (¼ pint) lukewarm water* ‖ *100 g (3½ oz) Italian 00 flour or strong white flour* ‖ *1 teaspoon olive oil* ‖ **DAY 2** *5 g (¼ oz) fresh yeast or ¼ teaspoon dried yeast* ‖ *125 ml (4 fl oz) lukewarm water* ‖ *150 g (5 oz) Italian 00 flour or strong white flour, plus extra for dusting* ‖ *½ teaspoon salt* ‖ *2 teaspoons olive oil, plus extra for oiling* ‖ *5 sun-dried tomatoes in oil, drained and cut into thick strips*

ONE On day 1, dissolve the yeast in a bowl with the sugar and measurement water. Add the flour and oil and stir the mixture until well combined. Cover with clingfilm and leave to stand for 24 hours. **TWO** On day 2, dissolve the yeast in the measurement water. Pour into the bowl with the starter dough and add the flour, salt and half the oil. Stir the mixture until well combined. Knead the dough on a floured work surface for 10 minutes until smooth and elastic, then place in an oiled bowl. Cover with a moist cloth and leave to rise in a warm place for 1½ hours until doubled in size. **THREE** Transfer the dough to a floured work surface and stretch it into a strip, 45 cm (18 inches) long. Scatter half the tomatoes over the central third of the dough, then fold the left-hand third of dough into the middle, covering the tomatoes. Press down with the heel of your hand to seal, then scatter this section of dough with the remaining tomatoes. Bring the right-hand dough over to cover the tomatoes and press to seal. Lightly flour a baking sheet and place the dough in the centre. Cover with a moist cloth and leave to rise in a warm place for 1 hour. **FOUR** When the dough feels soft and pillowy to the touch, place a roasting tin filled with water at the bottom of a preheated oven, 220°C (425°F), Gas Mark 7, which will help give the bread a good crust. Drizzle the top of the bread with the remaining oil, then dust lightly with flour. Bake for 25–27 minutes or until the base sounds hollow when tapped. Leave to cool on a wire rack.

Makes 1 large loaf

NUTRIENT ANALYSIS PER SLICE (1 LOAF = 12 SLICES) 456 kJ – 108 kcal – 3 g protein – 16 g carbohydrate – 1 g sugars – 4 g fat – 1 g saturates – 1 g fibre – 63 mg sodium

HEALTHY TIP The fat content of this bread is higher than that of plainer breads, so there are more calories per slice than in a lower fat bread.

Red onion and sage focaccia
Numerous toppings can be added to the basic focaccia base or kneaded into the dough for the final rising. This combination is delicious served with a selection of *antipasti*. Another topping to try is cherry tomatoes and anchovy, or keep it simple and classic with sprigs of rosemary.

INGREDIENTS *15 g (½ oz) fresh yeast or 1½ teaspoons dried yeast* ‖ *large pinch of caster sugar* ‖ *225 ml (7½ fl oz) lukewarm water* ‖ *350 g (11½ oz) Italian 00 flour or plain flour, plus extra for dusting* ‖ *½ teaspoon salt* ‖ *2 tablespoons olive oil, plus extra for oiling* ‖ *6 sage leaves, roughly chopped* ‖ *½ small red onion, finely sliced* ‖ *coarse sea salt*

ONE Dissolve the yeast in a bowl with the sugar, measurement water and half the flour. Cover with a moist cloth and leave to stand in a warm place for 15 minutes. **TWO** Stir the salt into the remaining flour, then tip the flour mixture into the now-foamy paste. Add 1½ tablespoons of the oil and stir the mixture with one hand until the ingredients are combined. Knead the dough on a floured work surface for 10 minutes until smooth and elastic. The dough should be very soft and slightly sticky. If it is too sticky to knead, add a little extra flour. Place the dough in an oiled bowl. Cover with a moist cloth and leave to rise in a warm place for 1 hour until doubled in size. **THREE** Knead half the sage and onion into the dough and transfer it to a lightly oiled baking sheet, about 30 x 20 cm (8 x 12 inches). Stretch it to fill the sheet, then cover with a moist cloth and leave to rise in a warm place for 30 minutes. Using your fingers, make deep dimples in the surface of the dough. Scatter with the remaining sage and onion, drizzle the top of the bread with the remaining oil, cover again and leave to rise in a warm place for 15 minutes until soft and pillowy to the touch. **FOUR** Season the top with coarse sea salt, then bake in a preheated oven, 200°C (400°F), Gas Mark 6, for 20 minutes or until the base sounds hollow when tapped. Transfer to a wire rack to cool. Eat warm or at room temperature.

Makes 1 large loaf

NUTRIENT ANALYSIS PER SLICE (1 LOAF = 12 SLICES) 505 kJ – 119 kcal – 4 g protein – 23 g carbohydrate – 1 g sugars – 2 g fat – 0 g saturates – 1 g fibre – 1 mg sodium

HEALTHY TIP The sodium content of bread can be quite high, so be careful how much salt you add to the mix. A high proportion of salt in the diet can cause blood pressure to rise.

Pizza marinara

Marinara should really just be pizza with a light tomato and oregano sauce, but because of its name, it is often mistaken for a seafood pizza. In that vein, this version is with anchovies and black olives, but if you want to be traditional, simply leave them out.

INGREDIENTS *1 quantity Basic Pizza Dough* (see page 15) ║ *200 ml (7 fl oz) passata* ║ *¼ teaspoon dried oregano* ║ *pinch of crushed dried red chillies* ║ *2 garlic cloves, crushed* ║ *plain flour, for dusting* ║ *8 anchovy fillets in salt or olive oil, well-rinsed or drained and halved lengthways* ║ *12 pitted black olives, halved* ║ *olive oil, for glazing* ║ *salt*

ONE Make the pizza dough following the method on page 15. **TWO** To make the topping, combine the passata, oregano, chillies and garlic in a bowl. Season with salt, cover and leave to allow the flavours to develop for 15 minutes. **THREE** Place a baking sheet in a preheated oven at its highest setting. Place one dough ball on the base only of a 23 cm (9 inch) loose-bottomed tart tin dusted with plenty of flour. Push down on the dough with your fingertips, spreading it into a round the same size as the tin base, leaving the border slightly thicker. If you get any tears, forcefully pinch the dough around the hole back together. **FOUR** Spoon 2–3 tablespoons of the tomato mixture over the pizza base, then arrange 4 anchovy halves on top. Scatter with a quarter of the olives and brush the border of the pizza with oil, to glaze. Remove the heated baking sheet from the oven, slide the tin base on to it, then quickly return to the oven. Bake for 7–8 minutes until crisp and risen. Serve immediately. As the first pizza cooks, you can be preparing the next one for the oven.

Makes 4 pizzas

NUTRIENT ANALYSIS PER SERVING 2120 kJ – 500 kcal – 15 g protein – 102 g carbohydrate – 4 g sugars – 7 g fat – 1 g saturates – 6 g fibre – 1173 mg sodium

HEALTHY TIP Pizza can be quite high in salt, from the salt in the dough and from the toppings. To reduce the salt content of this pizza rinse the olives and the anchovies thoroughly before use to remove any remaining brine.

Pizza pockets with Swiss chard and raisins

Swiss chard is similar to spinach in flavour, but more robust in texture. These pizza pockets are a real vegetarian treat and, served with a green salad, make a substantial meal.

INGREDIENTS *1 quantity Basic Pizza Dough (see page 15)* ‖ *1 kg (2 lb) Swiss chard* ‖ *2 teaspoons olive oil, plus extra for glazing* ‖ *2 garlic cloves, thinly sliced* ‖ *large pinch of crushed dried red chillies* ‖ *2 tablespoons raisins* ‖ *150 g (5 oz) mozzarella cheese (drained weight), roughly chopped* ‖ *plain flour, for dusting* ‖ *salt*

ONE Make the pizza dough following the method on page 15. **TWO** To prepare the Swiss chard, trim off the white stalk and cut the leafy part into 2.5 cm (1 inch) strips. Cook the strips in a saucepan of boiling water for 3–4 minutes until just tender, then drain thoroughly. Squeeze the chard between your hands to remove any excess moisture. **THREE** Heat the oil in a large frying pan over a low heat. Add the garlic, chillies and raisins and cook, stirring, for 1 minute. Add the Swiss chard, season lightly with salt and cook, stirring, for 2–3 minutes. Leave to cool, then stir in the mozzarella. **FOUR** Place a baking sheet in a preheated oven at its highest setting. Place one dough ball on the base of a 23 cm (9 inch) loose-bottomed tart tin dusted with flour. Spread the dough into a round the same size as the tin base with your fingertips. If you get any tears, forcefully pinch the dough around the hole back together. **FIVE** Spoon a quarter of the filling over half the pizza base, leaving a 1 cm (½ inch) border. Fold the empty dough over the filling to make a half-moon shape then press the edges firmly together. Seal the edges tightly by folding over into a scrolled pattern, then lightly brush the top of the pizza with oil, to glaze. **SIX** Remove the heated baking sheet from the oven, slide the tin base on to it, then quickly return to the oven. Bake for 16–18 minutes until crisp. Serve immediately. As the first pizza cooks, you can be preparing the next one for the oven.

Makes 4 pizza pockets

NUTRIENT ANALYSIS PER SERVING 2759 kJ – 650 kcal – 27 g protein – 118 g carbohydrate – 15 g sugars – 12 g fat – 5 g saturates – 6 g fibre – 1258 mg sodium

HEALTHY TIP The raisins in this pizza provide a good source of iron and some other minerals and vitamins. Swiss chard is a good source of B vitamins and, with the raisins, increases the fibre content of the pizza.

Pizza with grilled aubergine, basil and ricotta

The combination of delicious grilled aubergine, basil and ricotta ensures that this low-fat pizza topping is fresh and exciting. You can vary the topping by using griddled courgettes or roasted peppers instead of, or as well as, the aubergines.

INGREDIENTS *1 quantity Basic Pizza Dough (see page 15)* ‖ *125 g (4 oz) ricotta cheese* ‖ *150 ml (5 fl oz) passata* ‖ *5 large basil leaves, torn* ‖ *1 garlic clove, crushed* ‖ *2–3 small–medium aubergines* ‖ *plain flour, for dusting* ‖ *75 g (3 oz) mozzarella cheese (drained weight), roughly chopped* ‖ *olive oil, for glazing* ‖ *salt*

ONE Make the pizza dough following the method on page 15. **TWO** Using a fork, break the ricotta into olive-sized chunks, cover and refrigerate until needed. Combine the passata, basil and garlic in a bowl. Season lightly with salt, cover and leave for the flavours to develop while you grill the aubergines. **THREE** Slice the aubergines lengthways into 5 mm (¼ inch) slices. Heat a ridged cast-iron griddle pan over a high heat until it is searing hot, add the aubergine slices and cook for 2 minutes on each side until charred on the outside and soft all the way to the centre. If the outside is colouring too quickly, reduce the temperature to give the centre a chance to cook. Set aside. **FOUR** Place a baking sheet in a preheated oven at its highest setting. Place one dough ball on the base only of a 23 cm (9 inch) loose-bottomed tart tin dusted with plenty of flour. Push down on the dough with your fingertips, spreading it into a round the same size as the tin base, leaving the border slightly thicker. If you get any tears, forcefully pinch the dough around the hole back together. **FIVE** Spoon 2 tablespoons of the tomato mixture over the pizza base, top with a quarter of the aubergines, then scatter with a quarter each of the mozzarella and ricotta. Brush the border of the pizza with oil, to glaze. Remove the heated baking sheet from the oven, slide the tin base on to it, then quickly return to the oven. Bake for 7–8 minutes until crisp and risen. Serve immediately. As the first pizza cooks, you can be preparing the next one for the oven.

Serves 4

NUTRIENT ANALYSIS PER SERVING 2418 kJ – 570 kcal – 21 g protein – 104 g carbohydrate – 6 g sugars – 11 g fat – 5 g saturates – 7 g fibre – 657 mg sodium

HEALTHY TIP Traditional pizza can have a very high fat content. Both ricotta and mozzarella have a lower fat content than many cheeses, keeping the level of total and saturated fat down.

Pizza with cherry tomatoes, mozzarella and rocket
Fresh pizza toppings are perfect for a hot summer's day. Here, the sweetness of the milky mozzarella contrasts beautifully with the peppery wild rocket.

INGREDIENTS *1 quantity Basic Pizza Dough (see page 15) ‖ 200 g (7 oz) cherry tomatoes ‖ 2 garlic cloves, crushed ‖ large pinch of crushed dried red chillies ‖ 2 tablespoons olive oil, plus extra for drizzling ‖ 150 g (5 oz) buffalo mozzarella cheese, drained ‖ plain flour, for dusting ‖ 50 g (2 oz) wild rocket ‖ salt*

ONE Make the pizza dough following the method on page 15. **TWO** To make the topping, place the tomatoes in a large bowl and crush them between your fingers. Add the garlic and chillies, then stir in half the oil. Season with salt, cover and leave to allow the flavours to develop for at least 30 minutes while the dough rises. Tear the mozzarella into large pieces and set aside. **THREE** Place a baking sheet in a preheated oven at its highest setting. Place one dough ball on the base only of a 23 cm (9 inch) loose-bottomed tart tin dusted with plenty of flour. Push down on the dough with your fingertips, spreading it into a round the same size as the tin base, leaving the border slightly thicker. If you get any tears, forcefully pinch the dough around the hole back together. **FOUR** Spoon a quarter of the tomato mixture over the pizza base, then brush the border with oil, to glaze. Remove the heated baking sheet from the oven, slide the tin base on to it, then quickly return to the oven. Bake for 7–8 minutes until crisp and risen. Scatter with a quarter each of the mozzarella and rocket and serve immediately. As the first pizza cooks, you can be preparing the next one for the oven.

Makes 4 pizzas

NUTRIENT ANALYSIS PER SERVING 2580 kJ – 610 kcal – 23 g protein – 102 g carbohydrate – 5 g sugars – 15 g fat – 6 g saturates – 6 g fibre – 746 mg sodium

HEALTHY TIP Tomatoes contain all the antioxidant vitamins – A (betacarotene), C and E – plus the antioxidant mineral zinc. This makes them an extremely powerful preventative food medicine, strengthening the immune system against infection and lowering the risk of cataracts, heart disease, stroke and various forms of cancer.

Dolci – desserts

Blood orange granita

Blood orange has a unique bittersweet taste that makes the most delicious granitas and sorbets. Use Campari if you want to accentuate its bitterness, or opt for grappa to bring out the sweetness in the fruit and also give the granita an extra kick.

INGREDIENTS *400 ml (14 fl oz) freshly squeezed blood orange juice (about 4–5 oranges)* ‖ *grated rind of 1 blood orange* ‖ *75 g (3 oz) caster sugar* ‖ *2 tablespoons Campari or grappa*

ONE Heat half the orange juice with the rind and sugar in a small saucepan over a medium heat, stirring until the sugar has dissolved. Remove from the heat and stir in the remaining orange juice and the Campari or grappa. **TWO** Pour the mixture into a shallow, freezerproof dish in which the liquid should be about 2.5–3.5 cm (1–1½ inches) deep. Leave to cool to room temperature, then freeze for 40 minutes. **THREE** Beat the frozen granita mixture with a fork, to break up the ice crystals, then return to the freezer for 30 minutes. Repeat twice more until completely frozen. Stir well with a fork just before serving. Serve in individual bowls or glasses. The granita is best eaten on the day it is made.

Serves 4

NUTRIENT ANALYSIS PER SERVING 535 kJ – 126 kcal – 1 g protein – 30 g carbohydrate – 30 g sugars – 0 g fat – 0 g saturates – 0 g fibre – 2 mg sodium

HEALTHY TIP Oranges are rich in vitamin C, potassium, carotene and lutein. They are an ideal way to achieve a recommended daily allowance of vitamin C, as well as good for fighting colds, lowering cholesterol and providing anti-cancer properties.

Granita *al caffe*

This granita depends on good, strong espresso for its success. It is usually served with a dollop of whipped cream, but it can also be eaten plain as a mid-afternoon or after-lunch pick-me-up. Don't worry if the espresso seems too sweet at first, as freezing will dull the sweetness.

INGREDIENTS *65 g (2½ oz) caster sugar* ‖ *450 ml (¾ pint) espresso coffee* ‖ *whipped cream, to serve (optional)*

ONE Stir the sugar into the coffee while it is still warm. Take a sip and add more sugar to taste. **TWO** Pour the mixture into a shallow, freezerproof dish in which the liquid should be about 2.5–3.5 cm (1–1½ inches) deep. Leave to cool to room temperature, then freeze for 45 minutes. **THREE** Beat the frozen granita mixture with a fork, to break up the ice crystals, then return to the freezer for 20 minutes. Repeat twice more until completely frozen. Stir well with a fork just before serving. Serve plain or with a dollop of whipped cream in individual bowls or glasses. The granita is best eaten on the day it is made.

Serves 4

NUTRIENT ANALYSIS PER SERVING 280 kJ – 66 kcal – 0 g protein – 17 g carbohydrate – 17 g sugars – 0 g fat – 0 g saturates – 0 g fibre – 1 mg sodium

HEALTHY TIP If you do want to add cream to the granita consider using whipping cream (40% fat) instead of double cream (50% fat). You could also try crème fraîche (40% fat), or low-fat crème fraîche (15% fat).

Peach and white wine sorbet

Macerating or poaching peaches in white wine is very common in Italy, and turning it into a sorbet is the next logical step. If you can't find ripe peaches, leave the fruit out of the refrigerator for 3–4 days before making the sorbet.

INGREDIENTS *40 g (1½ oz) caster sugar* ‖ *3 tablespoons boiling water* ‖ *grated rind and juice of ½ lemon* ‖ *75 ml (3 fl oz) white wine* ‖ *700 g (1 lb 6 oz) ripe peaches, skinned and stoned* ‖ *1 peach, stoned and cut into thin wedges*

ONE Place the sugar in a heatproof jug. Pour over the measurement water and stir until the sugar has started to dissolve. Pour in the lemon juice and rind and wine and stir well until all the sugar has dissolved. Leave to cool to room temperature. **TWO** Purée the peaches in a food processor or blender until smooth, then stir into the cooled liquid. Pour the mixture into a shallow, freezerproof container and cover with clingfilm. Chill for 30 minutes. **THREE** Churn in an ice-cream machine following the manufacturer's instructions. Alternatively, freeze in the same container, beating the sorbet with a whisk at 45-minute intervals, until almost completely frozen, then process the sorbet in a food processor or blender until smooth. Freeze until solid. Transfer to the refrigerator for 10 minutes before serving to soften slightly, then serve with the peach wedges in individual bowls or glasses. The sorbet is best eaten on the day it is made.

Serves 4

NUTRIENT ANALYSIS PER SERVING 485 kJ – 114 kcal – 2 g protein – 25 g carbohydrate – 25 g sugars – 0 g fat – 0 g saturates – 4 g fibre – 3 mg sodium

HEALTHY TIP Peaches are a good source of vitamin C and also provide carotene and useful amounts of the B vitamins. Eating the sorbet on the day it is made ensures that the vitamin content does not deteriorate.

Strawberries with balsamic vinegar

This dessert takes seconds to put together. You will need sweet, juicy strawberries and top-quality syrupy balsamic vinegar, since the sweeter the raw ingredients, the less sugar you will need to add.

INGREDIENTS *500 g (1 lb) strawberries, hulled and halved‖ 2½ tablespoons good-quality balsamic vinegar ‖ 5 mint leaves, roughly chopped ‖ caster sugar, to taste ‖ 200 g (7 oz) ricotta cheese ‖ ½ tablespoon lemon juice ‖ 1 teaspoon clear honey*

ONE Gently combine the strawberries, balsamic vinegar and mint in a large bowl. Add sugar to taste, cover with clingfilm and leave to macerate in the refrigerator for 1 hour. Gently stir from time to time to combine the flavours. **TWO** Mash the ricotta in a bowl with a fork, then stir in the lemon juice and honey. Cover with clingfilm and refrigerate until ready to serve. **THREE** Serve the strawberries and their syrup in dessert bowls with a dollop of the flavoured ricotta.

Serves 4

NUTRIENT ANALYSIS PER SERVING 495 kJ – 119 kcal – 6 g protein – 12 g carbohydrate – 12 g sugars – 6 g fat – 4 g saturates – 3 g fibre – 62 mg sodium

HEALTHY TIP Ounce for ounce, strawberries contain more vitamin C than citrus fruit. It is thought that foods rich in vitamin C may lower the risk of cancers of the gastrointestinal tract.

Affogato al caffe This instant dessert combines two of the things Italians do best – coffee and ice cream. It doesn't necessarily need to be served with anything else, but you could spice it up a little by making your espresso *corretto*, that is with the addition of a dash of grappa, or by also bringing some Zesty Biscotti (*see page 156*) to the table when you serve.

INGREDIENTS *8 scoops of low-fat vanilla ice cream* ‖ *4 freshly made espresso coffees*
TO SERVE *grappa (optional)* ‖ *Zesty Biscotti (see page 156) (optional)*

ONE You will need 4 cappuccino cups or dessert bowls. Place 2 scoops of ice cream into each. **TWO** Pour a freshly made espresso over each cup or bowl and serve immediately.

Serves 4

NUTRIENT ANALYSIS PER SERVING 603 kJ – 144 kcal – 4 g protein – 17 g carbohydrate – 16 g sugars – 7 g fat – 2 g saturates – 0 g fibre – 1 mg sodium

HEALTHY TIP We drink coffee for the taste and the caffeine 'jolt', but freshly made coffee is also quite a good source of riboflavin. Riboflavin is one of the B-group vitamins, which act as 'co-factors' to make the body's enzyme systems work properly.

Fruit salad with sugar and lemon

Macerating the fruit in lemon and sugar draws out the juices from the fruit, creating a lovely lemony fruit syrup. Use any combination of your favourite ripe fruit, changing the selection depending on what is seasonally available in your area.

INGREDIENTS *250 g (8 oz) strawberries, hulled* ‖ *1 banana, peeled* ‖ *1 peach, halved and stoned* ‖ *1 pear, cored* ‖ *handful of green or red grapes* ‖ *3 tablespoons lemon juice* ‖ *2 teaspoons caster sugar*

ONE Halve the strawberries, then cut the remaining fruit into similar-sized pieces. **TWO** Gently combine the fruit in a large bowl with the lemon juice and sugar, cover with clingfilm and leave to macerate in the refrigerator for 1 hour. Gently stir the fruit from time to time to combine the flavours. Spoon into individual bowls or glasses and serve.

Serves 4

NUTRIENT ANALYSIS PER SERVING 343 kJ – 80 kcal – 1 g protein – 20 g carbohydrate – 19 g sugars – 0 g fat – 0 g saturates – 3 g fibre – 6 mg sodium

HEALTHY TIP Fruit salad will taste nicer if allowed to macerate for a period, but try not to cut up fruit or vegetables too long before serving or cooking as, once cut, enzyme action will gradually reduce the vitamin content of the fruit.

Ricotta and candied peel cake

This moist, fluffy teacake is as low in fat as they come and therefore a great option if you're watching your waistline. Look out for top-quality candied peel sold in large pieces – it is generally tangier and less sugary than the ready-chopped peel sold in tubs.

INGREDIENTS *300 g (10 oz) ricotta cheese* ‖ *3 eggs, separated* ‖ *250 g (8 oz) caster sugar* ‖ *275 g (9 oz) plain flour* ‖ *75 g (3 oz) mixed candied peel, roughly chopped* ‖ *finely grated rind of 1 lemon* ‖ *1 tablespoon baking powder* ‖ *2 tablespoons semi-skimmed milk* ‖ *butter, for greasing* ‖ *icing sugar, for dusting (optional)*

ONE Mash the ricotta in a large bowl with a fork, then vigorously beat in the egg yolks, working the mixture together for 2 minutes. Add the sugar and beat thoroughly once more. Fold in the flour, candied peel, lemon rind and baking powder. Loosen the mixture by stirring in the milk. **TWO** Whisk the egg whites in a separate bowl until they just hold their shape, then stir a quarter into the cake mixture. Gently fold in the remaining egg whites. **THREE** Line the base of a 23 cm (9 inch) nonstick loose-bottomed cake tin with greaseproof paper. Pour in the cake mixture and bake in a preheated oven, 180°C (350°F), Gas Mark 4, for 35–40 minutes or until firm and a skewer inserted into the centre of the cake comes out clean. Leave the cake to cool in the tin on a wire rack. Serve while still slightly warm, with a light dusting of icing sugar, if you like. Because of its low fat content, this cake should be eaten on the day it is baked.

Serves 10

NUTRIENT ANALYSIS PER SERVING 1227 kJ – 290 kcal – 8 g protein – 54 g carbohydrate – 32 g sugars – 6 g fat – 3 g saturates – 1 g fibre – 260 mg sodium

HEALTHY TIP Using ricotta cheese in this recipe means this cake has a comparatively low fat content.

Pecorino, pears and honey

Semi-matured or 'young' pecorino is often served as a dessert, accompanied by fruit and honey. The perfect stage of maturity is when the texture of the cheese is beginning to become crumbly yet still feels moist to the palette, and its nutty flavour retains some of the sweetness of a fresh cheese. Pecorino is particularly delicious when paired with Tuscan or Umbrian chestnut honey, or try a good-quality orange blossom honey.

INGREDIENTS *2 ripe pears, cut into thin wedges and cored* ‖ *200 g (7 oz) young pecorino cheese, shaved* ‖ *clear honey (ideally chestnut), for drizzling*

ONE Divide the pear wedges and pecorino slices between 4 dessert plates. **TWO** Drizzle with honey and serve immediately.

Serves 4

NUTRIENT ANALYSIS PER SERVING 1096 kJ – 226 kcal – 12 g protein – 18 g carbohydrate – 18 g sugars – 17 g fat – 10 g saturates – 1 g fibre – 1454 mg sodium

HEALTHY TIP Honey contains the monosaccharide (simple sugar) fructose, which is also present in fruits.   Fructose is the sweetest sugar known, which is why small quantities of honey can provide a very sweet taste.

Sorbetto al limone with wild strawberries

The lemon sorbet you get in Italian *gelaterie* or ice-cream parlours is far superior to anything you can buy in tubs. It is as fresh and tangy as the fruit itself and nothing is more invigorating on a scorching summer's day. It is especially delicious served with fragrant wild strawberries.

INGREDIENTS *125 g (4 oz) caster sugar* ‖ *5 tablespoons boiling water* ‖ *500 ml (17 fl oz) freshly squeezed lemon juice (about 10 lemons)* ‖ *wild strawberries, to serve*

ONE Place the sugar in a heatproof jug. Pour over the measurement water and stir until the sugar has started to dissolve. Pour in the lemon juice and stir well until all the sugar has dissolved. **TWO** Pour the mixture into a shallow freezerproof container and cover with clingfilm. Chill for 30 minutes. **THREE** Churn in an ice-cream machine following the manufacturer's instructions. Alternatively, freeze in the same container, beating the sorbet with a whisk at 45-minute intervals, until almost completely frozen. Process the sorbet in a food processor or blender until smooth. Freeze until solid. Transfer to the refrigerator 10 minutes before serving to soften slightly, then serve with a scattering of wild strawberries in individual bowls or glasses. The sorbet is best eaten on the day it is made.

Serves 4

NUTRIENT ANALYSIS PER SERVING 570 kJ – 134 kcal – 0 g protein – 35 g carbohydrate – 35 g sugars – 0 g fat – 0 g saturates – 0 g fibre – 2 mg sodium

HEALTHY TIP Like all the citrus fruits, lemons are an excellent source of vitamin C, which is essential for normal growth and repair of body tissue. Vitamin C also has antioxidant properties, which help to protect against cancer. Lemons also contain useful amounts of B vitamins.

Zesty biscotti

Cantuccini, as these biscuits are called in Italy, are a favourite after-dinner treat, to be dipped into coffee or a chilled glass of the dessert wine, Vin Santo. They are so moreish that it is lucky they are so low fat!

INGREDIENTS *100 g (3½ oz) plain flour, plus extra for dusting* ‖ *75 g (3 oz) caster sugar* ‖ *½ teaspoon baking powder* ‖ *¼ teaspoon vanilla extract* ‖ *1 egg, plus extra for glazing* ‖ *grated rind of 1 lemon* ‖ *grated rind of 1 orange* ‖ *pinch of salt* ‖ *½ tablespoon aniseed or fennel seeds*

ONE Place all the ingredients except the aniseed or fennel seeds in a food processor and process until the mixture begins to form a dough. Tip the dough out on to a lightly floured work surface and knead in the aniseed or fennel seeds. **TWO** Roll the dough out into a long snake shape about 3.5 cm (1½ inches) wide and transfer to a baking sheet lined with greaseproof paper. Brush lightly with beaten egg to glaze, then bake in a preheated oven, 180°C (350°F), Gas Mark 4, for 30 minutes. **THREE** Remove from the oven and reduce the oven temperature to 150°C (300°F), Gas Mark 2. Cut the dough diagonally into 1.5 cm (¾ inch) slices and lay the slices, cut side up, on the baking sheet. Bake for a further 45 minutes until the biscuits feel hard. Transfer to a wire rack to cool. The biscuits can be stored in an airtight container for up to 1 month.

Makes about 15 biscotti

NUTRIENT ANALYSIS PER SERVING 222 kJ – 52 kcal – 1 g protein – 11 g carbohydrate – 5 g sugars – 1 g fat – 0 g saturates – 0 g fibre – 22 mg sodium

HEALTHY TIP Fennel seeds are high in calcium and iron and make a tasty addition to baked products and soups or other savoury dishes. Aniseed seeds have less calcium than fennel seeds, but a higher iron content.

Index

Author acknowledgements

I would like to thank all the inspiring team of teachers at Tasting Places whom I have worked with. Carla Tomasi for her no-nonsense heart-warming cooking; Claudio Pecorari who can cook up a storm night after night without flinching; Sophie Brainsbridge whose easy, relaxed, unpretentious approach is what Italian cooking is all about; Maxine Clarke, for infecting me with her passion and giving me my first taste of Grapefruit and Campari granita; and Giuseppe Silvestri, who makes the best pizza outside Italy.

Thanks to the Hamlyn team, Emma Neish and Sunil Vijayakar for producing such a beautiful book.

Special thanks to friends and family who shared dinners with me, as we tasted the recipes in this book, especially Gina, who was practically on call from her kitchen in Rome, and Mô, who jumped in to help whenever necessary. Finally, of course, thanks to Nick – my favourite fresh Italian!

Picture acknowledgements

Special Photography: © **Octopus Publishing Group Limited**/Emma Neish

Other Photography: **Alamy**/Ian Evans/Adams Picture Library t/a apl 3 background, 5 right, 20 left, 42 left, 66 left, 88 left, 108 left, 128 left, 142 left

EXECUTIVE EDITOR Nicky Hill
PROJECT EDITOR Leanne Bryan
EXECUTIVE ART EDITOR Karen Sawyer
DESIGNER Miranda Harvey
SENIOR PRODUCTION CONTROLLER Manjit Sihra
PHOTOGRAPHY Emma Neish /© Octopus Publishing Group Ltd
FOOD STYLIST Sunil Vijayakar
PROPS STYLIST Liz Hippisley